International Relations

International Relations

Stephanie Lawson

polity

First published in 2003 by Polity Press in association with Blackwell Publishing Ltd

Reprinted 2007, 2008

Polity Press
65 Bridge Street Cambridge
CB2 lUR, UK

Polity Press
350 Main Street
Maiden, MA 02148, USA

A catalogue record for this book is available from the British Library.

Library of Congress Cataloging-in-Publication Data
Lawson, Stephanie.
  A short introduction to international relations / Stephanie Lawson.
    p. cm. - (Short introduction series)
  Includes bibliographical references and index. ISBN 978-0-7456-2959-9
    (hb : alk. paper) -ISBN 978-0-7456-2960-5 (pb : alk. paper)
  1. International relations. I. Title. 11. Series.
JZ1242 .L39 2003
327 - dc21   2002014154

Typeset in 10 on 12 pt Sabon
by SNP Best-set Typesetter Ltd., Hong Kong
Printed and bound in Great Britain by Biddles Ltd., King's Lynn, Norfolk

For further information on Polity, visit our website: http://www.polity.co.uk

Contents

Preface

This book provides a concise introduction to International Relations (IR) from both historical and contemporary viewpoints as well as from various theoretical approaches. It is written not just for students undertaking a first course in IR at a college or university, but also for those with a general interest in the subject matter of world politics. There is no one way to write such a book, as is evident when one looks at the various ways in which the contents of the many introductory IR texts that line the shelves of booksellers are selected and arranged. The approach taken in this book is one that seeks to tell the *story* of IR, from centuries before it was even recognized as an academic discipline in its own right – something that did not come about until the first part of the twentieth century. The narrative therefore offers a long historical overview. Chapter 1 sets out the domain of the subject, while chapters 2, 3 and 4 show how the theories and practices, ideas and institutions, have taken shape over the centuries to the present. Chapters 5, 6 and 7 focus more on selected thematic issues that are of particular concern at the time of writing. Both parts, however, are intimately related and the discussion in the first part of the book provides an essential background to the understanding of the thematic issues discussed in the final three chapters. In summary, the book provides a broad basis for further study rather than giving a detailed account of any particular branch of IR. Above all, this text is intended to engage and stimulate the critical interest of the reader in an immensely important area of study – one which deals with serious questions of life, and death, in the contemporary world.

To the extent that this book makes an intellectual contribution to the understanding of world politics, it is largely thanks to a number of friends and colleagues who, over the years, have helped me to think critically about politics and international relations from various viewpoints. I will remain forever grateful to Graham Maddox, Fred D'Agostino, Carolyn Nordstrom and Preston King for their friendship and for providing much intellectual stimulation over the years. I am also indebted to my colleague at the University of East Anglia, Mike Bowker, and the external readers for their very helpful comments and criticisms on the draft of this book.

SL

Introducing International Relations

This book has been written at a time when the world's political and economic contours are still in considerable flux following the end of the Cold War in the late 1980s and the subsequent collapse of the Soviet Empire in the early 1990s. Many have argued that the Cold War, which dominated the conduct of world politics for over four decades, also dominated the way in which people saw the world. Not only was there a dominant, overriding issue – the possibility of nuclear warfare between the superpowers and their allies – there seemed to be a dominant mode of analysing this state of affairs as well, and that was through a 'realist' lens. Times have changed. Nuclear warfare remains a threat, but it no longer seems likely to engulf the entire world. Alongside traditional concerns with war, there are now a great many other issues competing for equal attention. And although realist theories remain important, alternative approaches have become more prominent and most people are increasingly aware that there are many different ways of seeing the world. I start with some common conceptualizations of periods in world history, for these have a significant, if often imperceptible, influence on how one sees the world of International Relations (IR).

Eras in world politics

Although a new millennium has begun and the Cold War is fast receding into history, the events of 1945–89 are still seen as defining the present period, for this is still the 'post-Cold-War era'. This says something about the effect that the Cold War had not only on the perception of geopolitical relations but also on how people conceptualize and periodize the wider political world and its historical development in terms of large-scale structures, events and processes. Here it is interesting to note that, at the time, the Cold War era itself was generally referred to as the 'post-war' period while the years from 1918 to 1939 are known as the 'inter-war' period. Large-scale wars, whether hot or cold, therefore acted as defining moments in world politics throughout much of the twentieth century. Considering that that century is widely regarded as the bloodiest yet in terms of lives lost in warfare, this is probably appropriate.

Another way of conceptualizing the present period is by reference to the process of globalization. Although this phenomenon has been in evidence for decades, if not centuries, it has captured the public imagination in a way unmatched in any previous period. This may be partly explained by the fact that the end of the Cold War left a considerable vacuum to be filled. And the idea of globalization, which can be interpreted in many different ways according to various orientations to world politics, is an obvious candidate for filling much of that vacuum. The economic aspects of globalization, in particular, were given a huge boost by the collapse of socialism and the apparent triumph of capitalism, while it was widely assumed that liberal democracy was now the only legitimate form of government. The idea of globalization was also boosted by the rapid development in the 1990s of electronic communications, including the internet which, like many of the economic aspects of globalization, seemed to render borders meaningless.

A further important defining condition – one that has extended for several hundred years and which may be seen as providing the foundations for contemporary globalization – is modernity. For students of IR the beginnings of modernity are frequently traced to the seventeenth century when the sovereign state began to take shape. Modernity is also linked inextricably to technological and scientific development, the rise of industrialization and the (attempted) mastery of nature. In more general social and political terms, however, the beginnings of modernity can be traced back to the Renaissance and the rise of humanist thought, for this represented an early moment in the emancipation of thinking from the strictures of the medieval church. But it is most closely associated with the intellectual movement known as the Enlightenment which found practical expression in various revolutions against established authorities in Europe and the United States in the eighteenth and nineteenth centuries. In this context, modernity entails the rejection of traditional authority. Since it is progressive in character and embraces a positive vision of human emancipation from the grip of the past, it also has a strong normative dimension. Above all, modernity promotes the idea of universal human rationality and therefore feeds directly into the contemporary globalist project at both a technical and humanist level. Indeed, globalization may be seen as representing an advanced stage of modernity.

For some, all this is a 'good thing'. It means that a stage has been reached in the progressive history of humankind where it is advancing, in a more or less evolutionary sense, towards a higher and better stage of existence. For others, there are innumerable dangers lurking at every turn. Although the obliteration of humankind through global nuclear warfare (whether by immediate annihilation or through the longer-term effects of an ensuing nuclear winter) is less of a threat, 'advances' in modern science and technology carry threats to human existence in other ways. These range from the way in which carbon-based energy resources are exploited and consumed to the release of genetically modified plant and animal life into the biosphere with as yet unknown and possibly catastrophic consequences. Chemical and biological warfare constitute other obvious threats. But it is not just the physical environment that may be at risk. Others see the broader social, economic and political environment being threatened by a stultifying kind of globalized modernity destructive of diverse local cultures, values and lifestyles.

Having mentioned modernity at this early stage, I must also consider briefly some of the ideas associated with postmodernism for these have had a significant impact on the social sciences in recent years. Since postmodernism is intimately associated with how the world is represented, or how the world is seen, it is especially important to consider some of these ideas in the context of IR. The currency of the terms postmodern, postmodernity or postmodernism in contemporary usage owes much to architectural theory and practice. Postmodern ideas then found their way into literary theory, cultural studies, philosophy, history, educational studies and the social sciences. Postmodernity is also associated with a plethora of other 'posts', including the notion of post-industrial society. The prefix 'post' in postmodernism, incidentally, is generally used in the sense that 'the modern' has been transcended rather than indicating that the modern period has actually finished.

One of the best-known architects writing on the subject, Charles Jencks, has emphasized the introspective nature of the postmodern enterprise inasmuch as it demands a critical review of many deeply held assumptions. It is the kind of intellectual movement that rejects the rational certainties of modernity, and especially those 'meta-narratives' that claim the status of universal truths (see Jencks, 4/1996, esp. part 1). In place of singular truths and founts of authority, a postmodern intellectual stance requires recognition of a range of possible knowledges drawn from cultures and histories across the globe. Moreover, rather than accepting globalization as a massive unifying, homogenizing or integrating force that is working to mould the entire world in the image of the modern West, a postmodern disposition sees (and in some respects hopes for) a longer-term decline of Western hegemony, an increasing fragmentation of the global system and the establishment of multiple centres of authority. This is therefore a very different view of how the world might develop in the twenty-first century and beyond.

The domain of international relations

The discipline of IR is critically concerned with all the issues mentioned above and they are discussed more fully in the course of this book. But here, some basic definitional and conceptual issues must be addressed. The first concerns the very term 'international relations', what it is meant to denote and what images of the world it conveys. When capitalized, as in International Relations, and reduced to the acronym 'IR', it names a specific field of academic study taught in universities as a 'subject' or 'discipline'. It is closely related to politics – and is now in fact often referred to as 'world politics' – and is generally classified, along with political science as well as economics, sociology and anthropology, as a social science. But it has close relations with history, law and social philosophy as well. As a result, it stands at the intersection of varying intellectual and disciplinary strands of study. Some, however, would dispute its location at this intersection and insist that it belongs firmly to the more 'scientific' arena. This particular view reflects a bias towards a positivist interpretation of how the discipline – and the social sciences generally – should be understood. Another view repudiates the attempt at scientism, seeing it as a slavish and fruitless attempt to mimic the natural sciences, and emphasizes instead the importance of historical/interpretative approaches. Both have important implications for methodology. But before exploring the methodological issue, it is necessary to specify what the study of IR is supposed to encompass.

In its simplest and narrowest sense, IR is taken to denote the study of relations between states (that is, nation-states or sovereign states as distinct from states that make up a federal system like the US). In a somewhat broader sense, IR denotes interactions between state-based actors across state boundaries. This includes a variety of non-governmental actors and organizations. An intimately related concern is the state *system* as a whole which has been widely regarded as providing the essential foundation for international *order* which is, in turn, a prerequisite for justice. Whether one adopts the narrower or broader understanding, however, the central institution is still the state. Indeed, it could be said that the entire edifice of traditional IR is founded on the modern sovereign state.

This may seem straightforward enough. But there are not only many disputes about the proper objects of study and how these should be approached methodologically, there is disagreement as well about the terminology used even in naming the subject. This is in addition to disputes over such matters as the nature of sovereignty, the meaning of security, the notion of world order, the role of norms and values in the international sphere, the function of international institutions, the idea of humanity, the possibility of effective international law, what issues count as matters of 'international' concern, the relative importance of structures and agents in world politics, and so on. Not surprisingly, these disputes are reflected in conflicting theoretical and methodological perspectives. This raises the further question of what, exactly, is the purpose of studying IR. And again, there is more than one way of answering this question.

One recent text takes as its starting-point the structuring of the world into states: 'The main reason why we should study IR is the fact that the entire population of the world is divided into separate territorial political communities, or independent states, which profoundly affect the way people live' (Jackson and Sørenson, 1999, p. xv). This is a straightforwardly descriptive statement, but it says nothing about how people *ought* to live. In the same book, however, a more specifically normative purpose is expressed in the statement that IR 'seeks to understand how people are provided, or not provided, with the basic values of security, freedom, order, justice and welfare' (ibid., p. 2).

The first statement above assumes the absolute centrality of the state to the discipline of IR and therefore reflects a very traditional approach. The broad normative concerns articulated in the second statement, however, are very much in tune with the so-called 'new agenda' for IR in the contemporary period – an agenda that moves well beyond the strong focus on inter-state warfare (and its prevention) that characterized much work in IR in previous periods. The preface to an IR textbook written in the Cold War period, when the threat of catastrophic nuclear warfare on a global scale seemed very real, gives a clear example of this focus:

[A] Third World War, fought with nuclear weapons, would involve us all and destroy at least large areas on every continent. Policy planners as well as military strategists have never left any doubts about the seriousness of their deadly intentions ... The study of international relations is, therefore, hardly just an academic exercise – it is an investigation of the chances for our physical survival or rather scholars' and intellectuals' attempt to determine what can be done to avoid a collective disaster initiated by so-called political *elites* who act according to certain principles and pursue certain so-called national interests. (Krippendorff, 1982, p. vii)

The issue of war was the primary practical focus of IR throughout the twentieth century – but not just any type of war. Whereas war may be defined in terms of 'lethal intergroup violence' involving virtually any sort of group (Goldstein, 2001, p. 3), and without reference to geopolitical borders, the traditional focus of IR has been on inter-state warfare and its prevention. A further useful concept is 'war system', defined as 'the interrelated ways that societies organize themselves to participate in potential or actual wars', thereby constituting 'less a series of events than a system with continuity through time' (ibid.). The concern with war has not disappeared, but IR's 'new agenda' now embraces a vast range of policy issues. These encompass: global environmental concerns (which still include nuclear issues); the epidemiology of AIDS; legal and illegal migration, including refugee movements; the gap between the North and the South in terms of access to and consumption of resources; democratization and the full range of human rights from civil and political rights to the right to development; reform of the United Nations (UN) and its agencies; and the extension of international law and the prosecution of crimes against humanity, whether involving terrorism, religious fundamentalism or international organized criminal activities that range from drug production and trafficking to money laundering and the smuggling of all kinds of goods, including weapons, diamonds, endangered species and people.

The threat of major inter-state warfare was not regarded as a serious possibility for the first decade after the Gulf War (1991), but chronic instability in the Middle East and the increasingly aggressive and militaristic stance of the US and some of its key allies following the events of 11 September 2001 have given rise to much more cause for concern. There has also been the ongoing problem of 'internal conflicts' which continue to claim thousands of lives around the world each year and in which some of the worst basic human rights abuses, including torture, rape, mutilation and massacres of civilians, are perpetrated. Although supposedly contained within the confines of states, these conflicts have impacts well beyond their borders and are therefore recognized as matters of concern for international peace and security. Just one problem stemming from internal conflicts is the huge number of people who are either internally displaced or forced out as refugees. More generally, these conflicts are seen as having significant humanitarian dimensions for which the 'international community' has a moral responsibility to act or intervene in one way or another. More cynical observers would say that the 'international community' usually acts only when television cameras are around to convey images of human suffering to a global audience – the so-called CNN factor. Whatever its motivation, such action can take the form of simply establishing and running refugee camps, to efforts at international mediation, to physical intervention in the form of 'peace-keeping' and/or the implementation and enforcement of sanctions.

Internal conflicts usually involve a strong element of 'identity politics', in which religious, ethnic or cultural factors are seen as having a prime role to play in both instigating conflicts and maintaining their momentum. Mary Kaldor (1999, p. 6) defines identity politics as constituting 'a claim to power on the basis of a particular identity – be it national, clan, religious or linguistic'. In describing the violent conflicts arising from identity politics as part of the phenomenon of 'new wars', she contrasts the motivating forces with the geopolitical or ideological goals of earlier or 'old wars' where identity was linked more to state interests or forward-looking projects about how society might be better organized, rather than back to an idealized representation of the past (ibid., pp. 6–7). In recent years, conflicts in Northern Ireland, the Basque country, various parts of the Balkans, Chechnya, Israel/Palestine, Rwanda, Sri Lanka, Indonesia, Fiji and elsewhere have displayed distinct characteristics of identity politics. The violence involved has ranged from rioting and looting and a relatively small number of deaths in the case of Fiji to genocidal massacres of hundreds of thousands in Rwanda. A number of these conflicts involve claims to self-determination by minorities, sometimes in the form of greater autonomy for a group within the state. But just as often a claim to self-determination comes in the form of secession from an existing state in order to create a new one. Others may be based on a notion that one particular group has superior claims to control of an existing state. In all these instances, the state takes centre stage.

The possibility of culture wars on a regional or global scale has also been much discussed following the publication in 1993 of Samuel Huntington's provocative article on the 'clash of civilizations'. This was conceived as a successor to the great clash of ideologies of the Cold War period with the forces representing liberal democracy and capitalist economics on the one side and, on the other, the communist vision of how politics, economics and society ought to be organized for the greater good. While the author of another well-known article had heralded the triumph of liberal democracy and capitalism as the 'end of history', in the sense that the last great ideological dispute capable of inciting serious international conflict was over and done with (Fukuyama, 1989),

Huntington saw world history continuing in other, disturbing, ways. Of the civilizational entities that Huntington identified the most powerful, and the most likely to come into conflict with each other, were 'the West' on the one hand and an Islamic/Confucian alliance of forces on the other. A number of critics have dismissed Huntington's views as alarmist and/or based on false assumptions about the nature of identity politics and the role of culture in conflict. However, in view of the crises triggered by the attacks of 11 September 2001, purportedly in the name of Islam, Huntington's ideas may seem compelling. This is all the more reason to consider them with care.

To summarize this section, many of the issues and concerns touched on above, from the problems of environmental degradation to ethnic conflict, have obviously been around for decades, if not longer. But the difference now is that they are more widely recognized as issues of genuine concern for students of IR and for the international policy community. Global warming, for example, has at least as much currency as the possibility of large-scale inter-state warfare. For many places in Africa, the main threats to individuals and communities come not only from civil wars but also from disease. AIDS is the most publicized of these, but even more deadly in terms of loss of life in some areas are mosquito-borne diseases such as malaria. State security, moreover, is now rarely under serious threat from external forces. In places like Indonesia, Colombia, Solomon Islands, Sierra Leone and Spain, the main threats to the state come from within. In addition, many 'security' threats now loom in the form of environmental disasters, including a significant increase in the incidence and severity of natural disasters triggered by global warming. Since the end of the Cold War, these and other security concerns have come to the fore, so much so that the concept of security has been undergoing a major transformation. As described in chapter 5, the notion of 'human security' rather than 'state security' is now very much in the ascendance.

Approaches to the study of international relations

A common question arising from all the issues outlined above concerns the adequacy or appropriateness of conventional IR theories and approaches in tackling the items on this new agenda. The conventional theoretical foundations of the discipline as well as the dominant methodological approaches, although still finding much support among scholars and policy analysts, have become much more exposed to the critical glare of alternative approaches since the 1980s. Under 'conventional' theory is included liberalism and realism in both their classic forms as well as in more recent incarnations. Alternative approaches include feminism, constructivism, critical theory and postmodernism. In one way or another, these alternative positions have challenged both realist and liberal approaches, contributed fresh insights and expanded the intellectual space of the discipline. In chapter 5, I explain how each of these approaches has worked as a critique of both realist and liberal viewpoints on security in the contemporary period, for it is the issue of security that lies at the very heart of IR theory and practice and which therefore provides a key reference point for comparing and contrasting the different theoretical perspectives. But for introductory purposes, some of the main contours of realism and liberalism, as well of alternative approaches, will be sketched here.

The realist approach consists of a cluster of theories developed over the last sixty years or so, although many of its proponents claim that it has its roots in the writings of such luminaries as Thucydides, Machiavelli, Hobbes and Rousseau. There is no single coherent realist theory of international politics, but rather 'a common centre of philosophical gravity' in that international politics, as well as politics more generally, is viewed as a constant struggle for power and security (Frankel, 1996, p. x). Similarly, Jack Donnelly (2000, p. 9), while noting the absence of a single definition of realism, nonetheless identifies a realist research programme which emphasizes 'the constraints on politics imposed by human nature and the absence of international government'. A further key feature of realist thought is the emphasis on the way in which states negotiate the anarchic nature of the international political environment:

> From the beginning realism has offered explanations for how political units – today we call them states – protect and preserve themselves in an anarchic environment in which dangers to security and welfare are always present, and even survival itself is not assured. The pursuit by states of their own security and autonomy is impinged upon and limited by other states' pursuit of their . . . security and autonomy. The relationship among states is thus fundamentally and inalterably a conflictual relationship, with states constantly and continuously jostling with and elbowing each other as they try to improve their security and enhance their autonomy. This restless agitation is made more dangerous because of the anarchic nature of the international system: There is no superior arbiter of states' conflicting claims, and no superior authority with the ability to enforce arbitration rules. (Frankel, 1996, p. ix)

Realist theory as it developed from the 1930s did so at least partly as a reaction to, and a critique of, liberal internationalist theory of the inter-war years which realists branded as 'idealism'. But the so-called idealism of this period was only one manifestation of liberal ideology in the study of international politics. James L. Richardson (2000) shows that 'contending liberalisms' have been at work in world politics, as much as in 'domestic' politics, before and after the inter-war period. But as with realism, there are certain themes that remain constant, such as an emphasis on the value of economic freedoms (especially in international trade), support for national self-determination and a world of states organized and regulated according to norms and rules, respect for the doctrine of non-intervention while at the same time opposing authoritarian political rule within states in principle, and a preference for disarmament in security policy.

With respect to the study of gender in IR, the various feminist approaches range from liberal and socialist feminisms to radical, postcolonial and postmodern feminisms. But again, there is a common point of departure and that is that feminist critiques of IR's dominant approaches view these as irredeemably masculinist in their most basic assumptions. Jan Jindy Pettman, for example, argues that traditional IR is in fact one of the most masculinist of the social sciences, with its focus on the 'high politics' of diplomacy, war and statecraft which calls up 'a world of statesmen and soldiers' – in short a world in which the principal actors are male, notwithstanding the occasional emergence of women like Indira Gandhi, Golda Meir and Margaret Thatcher (Pettman, 2/2001, p. 583). With respect to realist IR's key concept, power, V. Spike Peterson and Anne Sisson Runyan argue that the 'gendered division of power makes possible not only the relative denial of formal power to women in the international system but also the exclusion of women's struggles and "women's issues" from the world politics agenda.' To see how this division operates as a mechanism of oppression, they say that two interrelated aspects of power need to be explored: 'the gendered nature of the concept of power (the lens) and the gendered effects of this concept of power (the different positioning of women and men)' (Peterson and Runyan, 2/1999, p. 113).

One of the most interesting questions that feminism raises concerns some taken-for-granted assumptions about 'human nature' – a concept that is deeply embedded in political theory in general and classical realism in particular. If a certain state of affairs is regarded as 'natural' or as inherent in 'human nature', such as a gender hierarchy in which males dominate, rather than simply the result of human construction or agency, there are substantial *political* consequences for social organization, including relations between communities or states. And while the hierarchy is ever accepted as natural, then the status quo of male privilege goes largely unchallenged (True, 1996, p. 213).

The constructed nature of social, economic and political institutions and practices more generally is, as the name suggests, a primary starting-point for constructivist approaches to IR. Once again, there are varying strands which, in the case of constructivism, include feminist variants, postmodern variants, statist variants, critical variants and so on. Generally speaking, constructivist approaches have emerged out of social theory and are a response to dissatisfaction with the failure of conventional theories to take account of the social aspects of the subject matter. According to one commentator, the major unifying element in the constructivist literature 'is a concern with explaining the evolution and impact of norms on national and international security' (Farrell, 2002, p. 72). In addressing the general epistemological approach which makes constructivism distinctive, another exponent explains that 'people always construct, or constitute, social reality, even as their being, which can only be social, is constructed for them' (Onuf, 1989, p. 1). Constructivists such as Nicholas Onuf, however, do not repudiate the reality of the material world, or always draw a sharp distinction between the social and ideational on the one hand, and the material on the other. Rather, they interact in complex and variable ways with neither the social nor the material 'defining each other out of existence' (ibid.). In further explanation of this approach, John Gerard Ruggie says that: 'Constructivists hold the view that the building blocks of international reality are ideational as well as material; that ideational factors have normative as well as instrumental dimensions; that they express not only individual but also collective intentionality; and that the meaning and significance of ideational factors are not independent of time and place' (Ruggie, 1998, p. 33).

Critical theory, like realism and liberalism, claims an intellectual heritage that stretches back over several centuries, drawing on the work of Hegel, Kant and Marx as well as Enlightenment philosophy more generally. Its twentieth-century roots, however, are usually associated with the Frankfurt School which nurtured such thinkers as Max Horkheimer, Herbert Marcuse, Theodor Adorno, Walter Benjamin and Jurgen Habermas (Devetak, 1996a, p. 147). There are some marked similarities between those who place their work within the general framework of critical theory on the one hand, and those who have adopted a constructivist approach. Some of the intersections are evident in the explanation of critical theory offered by Andrew Linklater (1996) who describes it as a strand of social theory which has four principal achievements. First, in rejecting positivism and the notion of 'objective reality', critical theory focuses attention on the social construction and effects of knowledge, especially with respect to the way in which unfair social arrangements may be produced and reproduced. Second, critical theory opposes the notion that the structure of the social world as we know it, including the structure of inequalities of wealth and power, is immutable. Third, in addressing issues of inequality, critical theory (especially through the work of Habermas) learns from and overcomes weaknesses inherent in Marxism, not by rejecting class or the mode of production as fundamental to social exclusion, but by extending the analysis to include other forms of exclusion (such as gender and race). Fourth, critical theory has the capacity to envisage new forms of community that break with unjustified exclusion, thereby challenging the moral significance of national boundaries with a view to looking at the possibilities of 'post-sovereign forms of political life' (Linklater, 1996, pp. 279–80). Critical theory therefore has an explicitly normative orientation that goes beyond a mere concern with explanation.

Of all the theoretical approaches in IR, postmodernism seems to be the one that is most difficult to define or summarize. As Richard Devetak points out, proponents of a postmodern approach disagree among themselves over the meaning and definition of postmodernism, as do its critics. Furthermore, the different understandings of postmodernism sometimes amount to fairly minor differences of emphasis, but in other cases the theoretical trajectories and conclusions may be very far apart (Devetak, 1996b, pp. 179–80). What one can say is that postmodernism (which is often taken to incorporate poststructuralism) is associated with the work of such thinkers as Friedrich Nietzsche, Martin Heidegger, Jacques Derrida and Michel Foucault, and is concerned with the relationships between knowledge and power. A common theme is the rejection of objective truth and, as a corollary, of firm foundations for knowledge, including moral knowledge. For this reason, postmodernists are frequently accused of embracing a radical form of ethical relativism or at least of offering only negative critiques of other foundational theories. Yet some postmodern writers within IR are deeply concerned with mounting an ethical critique of such constructions as sovereignty, especially in relation to the exclusionary practices associated with it (see, for example, Ashley and Walker, 1990; George, 1994). In this respect, they share at least some common ground with critical theorists.

Another new direction for IR in recent years, and one stimulated in part by the increasing influence of alternative viewpoints discussed above as well as dissatisfaction with the limitations imposed by conventional approaches, is the extent to which at least some IR scholars are now inclined to draw from other disciplines and sub-disciplines. At the same time, scholars from other disciplines are contributing substantially to debates and discussions that were once considered the preserve of IR. I have mentioned already the close relationship that IR has had with other social sciences as well as with history, law and social philosophy. In the contemporary world, with a major focus on international criminal activity – which includes both international organized crime as well as politically motivated crimes such as those commonly described as 'crimes against humanity'– the relationship between IR and international law is clearly an important one. The strength of contemporary studies in International Political Economy (IPE) is another indication that international politics cannot stand apart from economics. It must engage critically with it, especially if it is to provide a serious and worthwhile critique of important aspects of global distributive justice (see Higgott, 2002).

A further interesting interdisciplinary development has come about through the so-called 'cultural turn' in the humanities and in the social sciences. Not only has 'cultural studies' become established as a school of critical interdisciplinary learning within universities around the world, but studies in 'cultural sociology', 'cultural history', 'cultural geography', 'cultural politics' and 'legal cultures' are now commonplace. For anthropology, of course, culture has always been the master concept. Now it is being appropriated – some might say misappropriated – by scholars in other disciplines. Indeed, it has probably become the interdisciplinary concept *par excellence*. In IR and politics more generally, culture has been closely associated with identity politics. And since there has been such an upsurge of interest in this phenomenon in the post-Cold-War period, the culture concept has naturally been given a significant boost along with it. The increased interest in culture among IR scholars has also been seen as symptomatic of a more general opening up of the discipline after the Cold War. According to one commentator, 'a burst of critical scrutiny' in IR has meant that various 'partially convergent critical challenges [have] . . . instituted greater intellectual and sociological flexibility in IR scholarship' and a return of culture and identity is part and parcel of a 'moment of robust intellectual openness' (Lapid, 1996, p. 4).

Intellectual openness aside, it is important to question just how concepts such as 'culture' are to be understood in the context of IR. Earlier, I mentioned Huntington's 'clash of civilizations' thesis. His use of the culture concept in this context has been widely regarded by critics as simplistic. Other uses have tended to be somewhat naïve too, especially to the extent that they have taken up a very old-fashioned concept of culture developed in early twentieth-century cultural anthropology (but long since abandoned by many contemporary anthropologists themselves) and applied it quite uncritically in various analyses. This is also evident in some approaches to normative issues in IR.

Another point to consider in terms of new directions for IR, especially if much of the work does become increasingly interdisciplinary, is whether IR will simply dissolve as a subject in its own right with its main concerns thereafter being absorbed into a more amorphous collection of issues under the general heading of 'international studies' or 'world politics'. The latter is increasingly used as a replacement term since it is seen as allowing for a wider range of issues to be encompassed within it, and is therefore more appropriate for the contemporary period. John Baylis and Steve Smith, the editors of a book with both 'world politics' and 'international relations' in its title, say they have chosen to give prominence to the former term because their interest is 'in politics and political patterns in the world, and not only those between nation-states' (as is implied in the word 'international'). They go on to say that their interest is in relations between organizations that may or may not be states, for example, multinational companies, terrorist groups or non-government organizations (NGOs) such as those that deal with international human rights issues (Baylis and Smith, 2/2001, p. 2). Much the same viewpoint informs the present analysis and so I frequently use the term 'world politics' throughout this book when indicating the general subject matter of contemporary IR.

The term 'international studies' is more explicitly interdisciplinary than 'world politics'. In some understandings it is not based on any one discipline at all but can encompass insights from virtually any of the humanities and social sciences without necessarily assimilating these to a specifically political study of the world, or any particular part of it. International studies often incorporate area studies (e.g. South-East-Asian or European studies), which may include the study of languages, cultural practices, cross-cultural relations, history, geography and so on. These types of study obviously have much relevance for contemporary IR but, many would argue, do not necessarily lie at the core of its concerns, which must retain a focus on international or world *political* concerns.

The interest in and reasons for looking to 'world politics' and 'international studies' as alternative formulations for what IR scholars are supposed to be doing are very relevant matters to think about, especially in light of the various challenges that have been mounted with respect to the state, which is the entity on which the discipline of IR has been largely founded. It is time now to consider this latter issue in a little more detail. To begin, I turn next to the meaning of 'the international', for this is at the heart of a basic terminological dispute that has implications for how the state has been defined and located in IR.

Defining the international

The English legal and political theorist Jeremy Bentham (1748–1832) first coined the word 'international' in 1780. He was seeking an English equivalent for the Latin phrase *ius gentium*. While this translates more or less as 'the law of nations', Bentham was probably looking for something that captured more fully the dynamics associated with law as it operated *between* states and which were clearly distinguishable from law as it operated *within* states. In coining the word, and applying it to the sphere both outside and between states, Bentham reinforced the legal status of the sovereign nation-state as well as consolidating a political-legal distinction between 'the domestic' affairs of a state on the one hand and its relations with other states in a distinct sphere 'outside' the domestic on the other. Most importantly, as soon as the notion of the 'international' achieved consolidation as a concept through Bentham's neologism, the sovereign state itself could be fully conceptualized as the defining political unit for both the 'national' and the 'international'.

This distinction between inside/outside, national/international was accepted for many years as a reasonably accurate reflection of how world order is configured. But it has been criticized in more recent times for masking much more complex realities. Political, social and economic interactions taking place around the globe – beyond the sphere of the domestic – clearly involve much more than state-to-state relations. In international business, including finance, trade, manufacturing and so on, this seems obvious. In politics and at a social level, it may at first be less obvious, but there is nonetheless a great deal of activity that does not involve the state *per se*. NGOs are thriving as international actors in their own right. These include organizations involved in charitable aid, environmental issues, human rights, religious activities and peace advocacy as well as those devoted to less worthy ends, such as migration racketeering, money laundering, arms smuggling, the drug trade and terrorism. Given these developments, the very idea of 'international relations' may seem obsolete (Rosenau, 1990, p. 6).

The word 'international' has also attracted criticism for conveying the impression that 'nations' rather than 'states' actually do the interacting. The term 'United Nations' has been criticized for similar reasons. Although frequently conflated, the terms 'nation' and 'state' denote two quite different entities. But like many terms denoting complex concepts, there has been much contestation over adequate definitions. The former refers more or less to 'a people' which may be defined as 'a named community occupying a homeland, and having common myths and a shared history, a common public culture, a single economy and common rights and duties for all members' (Smith, 2001, p. 13). The concept of the state, in contrast, is defined in legal-institutional terms as 'a set of autonomous institutions, differentiated from other institutions, possessing a legitimate monopoly of coercion and extraction in a given territory' (ibid., p. 12). The combined term 'nation-state' reflects an ideal that has been at the heart of much theorizing about world order, at least as far as conventional IR is concerned. The ideal is that 'a nation' (understood as 'a people') should be matched to 'a state'. In other words, a nation for each state, and a state for each nation. This ideal, which has often been expressed in claims to 'self-determination', has proven to be one of the most controversial and difficult matters in the theory and practice of international relations in the modern period.

Despite the presence of ethnic minorities and immigrant communities in almost all countries around the world, a simple way of seeing the world is in terms of equating states with a singular people, for example, France with 'the French', Indonesia with 'Indonesians' and so on. Nationalism itself is an ideology of the state in so far as it identifies peoples with states. In a student atlas of world politics, the fourth edition of which was published in 2000, the first map, entitled 'Current World Political Boundaries', is introduced in terms that, not surprisingly, reflect this conventional approach: 'The international system includes states (countries) as the most important component. The boundaries of countries are the primary source of political division in the world, and for most people nationalism is the strongest source of political identification' (Allen, 4/2000, p. 2).

One's 'nationality' is therefore defined in terms of the state in which one lives, or comes from, and this may be regardless of one's origins or descent. This is especially so in the United States, Australia and, increasingly, Great Britain and other European states with substantial immigrant populations. But nationality can also be very closely tied to notions of race and culture, as is the case with Japan where third-generation Koreans, for example, cannot obtain formal citizenship and all the rights that go with that status.

Mapping the international

Looking at the contemporary world political map, which shows around 190 countries all with assigned names from Afghanistan to Zimbabwe, marked out in contrasting colours and with clearly drawn borders, it all seems quite familiar and natural. Unless, that is, you were born more than a couple of decades ago. In this case, you would remember when the map showed many fewer countries – especially in the area of the former Soviet Union – and the current map should therefore strike you as much more colourful and varied. If you were born, say, around the middle of the twentieth century, or before, you may also remember another version of the world political map that had numerous pink-coloured places all around the world, for this was the colour chosen to denote countries of the former British Empire – later transformed into the Commonwealth.

One of the most important lessons to be learnt from this is that there is nothing permanent about political boundaries. Nor is there anything necessarily 'natural' about them – even where a single country is conveniently situated within a self-contained geographical space like an island, or where the boundary between two countries follows the line of a river or mountain range. The construction of political boundaries does not follow an eternal law of nature that is indelibly inscribed on the surface of the globe. Boundaries, such as those that represent divisions between states, are *socio-political* constructs. This means that they have been devised by humans and reflect particular socio-political interests, needs, purposes and distributions of power at a given point in time. In this sense, states and their boundaries are often described as 'culturally and historically particular' entities, meaning that they emerged at a specific historical time in a specific socio-political context. This observation, which broadly underscores constructivist, critical theory and postmodernist approaches, serves as a corrective to theories that assume the universal and timeless character of the modern state. In summary, although states and their boundaries – as with any social or political institution – may certainly endure for very long periods, they cannot be regarded as permanent fixtures. Just as they were created by human agency in the past, so too can they be modified or dismantled by the same force in the present or future.

It is clear, then, that the boundaries of states, which form the basis of the 'international', are subject to change according to shifting circumstances. So too are their 'internal' political structures and regime types. The constitutional monarchy in Britain, the US presidential system, federal institutions from Nigeria to Australia, India, Canada, Germany and Russia – all are subject to transformation. And at the broadest level, the international state system itself is not immune to significant change either, as contemporary globalists are apt to point out. Even so, as a particular type of political community, the sovereign state model and the state system to which it has given rise have rarely been called into question throughout most of the modern period.

Internationalizing the state system

With the process of decolonization that followed the Second World War, there was no question that the former colonies would assume all the trappings of formal sovereign statehood, including eligibility for membership of the newly created United Nations along with the trappings of parliamentary or presidential democratic systems. 'Independence' was in fact just about exactly equivalent to attaining formal, recognized sovereign statehood in an international system of states. With the proliferation of new states in this period, decolonization can actually be seen as giving the formal institution of statehood a significant boost. Indeed, decolonization effectively brought about the internationalization of the modern state system in the second half of the twentieth century – some four hundred years after it emerged in Europe.

Given the nature of the colonial experience and the fact that independence was often achieved through struggle and sacrifice, it is hardly surprising that sovereign statehood was taken up with much enthusiasm in the former colonial world, and has been guarded jealously ever since. Nonetheless, sovereign statehood in terms of independence, while initially promising much, has delivered very little for many people in the former colonial world. And to the extent that they have possessed formal sovereign equality with countries of the First World (or the North) it has scarcely placed them on an equal footing in any other way. On the other hand, where the state appears to have failed in places such as Somalia, Sierra Leone and the Congo, even a poorly functioning state dependent on aid and loans may seem a more desirable alternative.

While colonial empires were declining and new sovereign states were emerging everywhere in the post-war period, the countries of Western Europe embarked on a quite different course. Here, the process of European regional integration or regionalization soon got under way. This process has been ongoing in terms of both depth and breadth. Many see it as bringing about fundamental changes in the nature of European states, especially in terms of the diminution of sovereign powers and autonomous political status. To the extent that the European Union (EU) is seen as a success in economic terms as well as in strengthening regional security, however, it has inspired other attempts at regional integration around the world from Latin America to South-East Asia and Africa (see, generally, Gamble and Payne, eds, 1996).

There is some irony in the fact that Western Europe is the birthplace of a form of regionalism that seems set to displace the sovereign state as a major component of world order. For it was here that the sovereign state first emerged as a form of political community. The standard historical point of reference is the Peace of Westphalia (1648), instituted after a period of warfare inspired largely by religious rivalries between Catholics and Protestants. The Westphalian agreement set out the template not only for the modern state but also for a form of order based on a state system for Europe. The principle of inviolable sovereignty was the most crucial element in the scheme. Around three hundred years later, and in the wake of the vicious war that had its epicentre not far from Westphalia, the European Movement began gathering sufficient momentum to bring about a significant undermining of the sovereignty principle in both theory and practice. As suggested above, the EU is now widely regarded as a model of successful regionalization to be emulated elsewhere. Whether regional blocs come to displace states as the principal units of world order, however, is another question.

Globalizing the international

Along with regionalization, the phenomenon of globalization has, of course, been touted by many as the principal dynamic that is transforming political and economic relations around the contemporary world. As a force that transcends the mere 'international' with its inescapably statist foundations, globalization is seen as undermining the traditional sovereign state, rendering its boundaries meaningless and its governments impotent in a post-Cold-War era of triumphant global capitalism. In this formulation the traditional tension between the state and the free market is resolved in favour of the latter. But is this really the case? Has state capacity really declined that much in terms of its control over economic and related issues? Or is there simply too much hype about hyper-globalism? Alternatively, was there ever a golden age in which the state, or at least some states, possessed genuine control over a national economy and virtually all key areas of political concern? Another question worth asking here is whether the possible withering away of the state in this manner is a 'good thing' or whether states with a reasonably strong capacity to regulate and govern remain important for issues of both order and justice.

A further aspect of contemporary globalism (a term that captures a variety of state-transcending themes) that must be considered concerns global governance. This is another phrase lacking any great precision in its application. What it does *not* mean, though, is a form of 'world government' whereby all political units in the world (i.e. states) come under the jurisdiction of a single effective governing authority. Notwithstanding the beliefs of some right-wing fringe organizations in the US and elsewhere whose members are convinced that the UN is the harbinger of an oppressive system of world government, the UN is nothing of the kind. Nor is it likely to be as long as one of its foundational principles remains the sanctity of the sovereign state system – even though this has been softened in the post-Cold-War period by an apparent willingness to engage in or endorse acts of 'humanitarian intervention' that may transgress the principle of state sovereignty.

Although lacking precision, the term 'global governance' denotes various methods of formal and informal global regulation that range from the United Nations and its many agencies to bodies such as the

World Trade Organization (WTO) and the organization of Multi-National Corporations (MNCs). These are part of what is frequently referred to as 'global economic governance'. But global governance more generally includes a variety of NGOs as well as diffuse social movements and normative regimes such as the international human rights regime. Indeed, behind many manifestations of global governance, especially of the latter kind, lies a distinct normative theme that puts a premium on the notion of a common humanity with common concerns, needs and interests. In short, the normative side of global governance denotes an orientation to the common good that transcends the 'international' as reflected in the mapping of state boundaries and the traditional emphasis on the principal of state sovereignty, and embraces instead a global ethic of order and justice. Both globalization as a process, and global governance as a set of formally and informally institutionalized practices, may therefore be seen to have absorbed or subsumed the 'international' within a larger framework denoted by the all-encompassing 'global'.

CONCLUSION

A major theme of this book concerns the profoundly normative nature of the IR discipline, which was formally constituted as a field of study in its own right in the aftermath of the First World War. The purpose of IR then was to study, in a very focused and concerted way, the causes of war and the conditions for peace so that the horrors of the kind of warfare experienced in 1914–18 would become past history on a permanent basis. Whatever methods, approaches and theories have been adopted in subsequent years, this normative purpose remains at the heart of the discipline.

There is no one best method of approaching the general field of IR or of organizing its subject matter. However, I have chosen to provide in the next chapter, first, an account of 'states in history' and, second, a more specific discussion of the development of the 'classical tradition' of IR scholarship through an account of the rise of the European state and the development of the international state system in the modern period. The 'states in history' approach is especially important for another of the main themes of this book, and that is that there is nothing fixed or eternal about any particular political or social formation.

2

States in History

The modern state has provided the basis for the study of IR since the discipline's inception. More generally, it has largely defined the way in which most people see the world and their place in it. Security and identity, being and belonging in the world – all are traditionally seen as very much wrapped up in the modern state as the major social and political institution enveloping people's lives. But what exactly is 'the state'? How and why did it come into being? What functions or purposes does it serve? Will it always hold centre stage as the principal political institution in national and international political organization? Or are there other institutions and forms of organization that are rendering the state increasingly irrelevant?

For many people, the state has been so taken for granted that it may not have occurred to them to pose these questions. In the present era, however, IR's fundamental institutions have been much debated and there has been increasing scepticism about the efficacy of the modern state and the wider international state system. The purpose of this chapter is not to address these issues in detail since they are the subject of chapter 7. Rather, it is to provide a broad historical view on how different states have developed from the time that humans first formed more or less settled communities up to the rise of the modern sovereign state and state system. Most importantly, it discusses how political *thought* about the state has developed over the centuries. The title of this chapter is the same as that of John A. Hall's edited collection (1986) and is intended to emphasize, as he and other historical sociologists do, the fact that states are not 'just there'. Furthermore, a broad historical study demonstrates that states are not simply products of modernity but are evident across most epochs and cultures (Ferguson and Mansbach, 1996, p. 275).

Defining the state

At its simplest, a state is a political community. This not only denotes a common political framework of customs, rules and other authoritative institutions, but also the designation of a certain group of people as living within and having ultimate control over a certain portion of the earth's surface. This means that there is a more or less discernible boundary between one political community and the next. Boundaries, whether social or geographical, need not be very rigid. Over the millennia, boundaries have in practice been permeable as well as moveable. Nonetheless, a defining element of the state is its bounded, territorial character. Those communities (such as nomadic ones) that do not have the same fixed relationship with a particular territory have usually been excluded from the definition of state, even though they do form a political community. So while all states may be defined as political communities, not all political communities take the form of states.

The modern state is not only a territorial entity associated with a particular group of people (the 'nation'), it embodies the principle of sovereignty as well. Sovereignty has two dimensions. In terms of internal political arrangements, sovereignty refers to the presence of a central, authoritative, supreme power that stands over and above all other forms of power within the state. In practice, this power is exercised by a government. With respect to the external environment of the state – that is, the international sphere – there is no authority higher than the individual states that make up the international system of states, and no individual state possesses a greater measure of sovereignty than any other. In formal terms, then, all states are equally sovereign in the international sphere and therefore formally equal in international law. However, to say that the Kingdom of Tonga is formally equal to the United States of America is one thing. To argue for their equality in any other way seems ludicrous.

I return to the modern sovereign state later. For the moment, it is important to note that there is not only great variety among contemporary states in terms of size, power, social structure, internal political arrangements, economic factors, geography, environment and other characteristics, there has also been a variety of state forms throughout history. The 'states in history' approach adopted here therefore seeks to show a sample of the variety of states from different times and different places. This approach highlights not only the variety of forms that states can take, but also the fact that there is nothing fixed or eternal about any particular form, including the present sovereign state form.

States and empires in the pre-modern world

The earliest forms of political community were nomadic hunter-gatherers who constituted small-scale bands often not much bigger than an extended family network. As mentioned above, although these groups certainly formed a type of political community, they did not have an attribute that is normally associated with states, namely, control of a fixed territory. This came with the development of agriculture which required a more permanent association with a particular portion of land. Evidence of settled existence stretches back only about five thousand years – a relatively short time in the history of the human species. Although early nomadic groups must have had mechanisms for mediating relationships with other such groups with whom they inevitably interacted, most writers on the subject of relations between political communities (i.e. international relations) do not regard these as coming within their purview. Rather, the starting-point for such analyses comes with the settling of people in fixed places. These provided the basis not only for states as such, but state *systems* as well. In addition, permanent settlement provided the foundation for 'civilization', a term that has been invested with a variety of meanings and nuances.

The remains of ancient civilizations, as well as smaller political communities that either became constituent parts of empires or existed independently, are found throughout the world. Not all left written records, but even the orally preserved histories of some, such as the island societies of Polynesia, together with archaeological material, provide quite a detailed insight into their early socio-political systems as well as some idea of the relations between different political communities in the region. The Aztec and Inca civilizations of Pre-Columbian Meso-America and Andean America respectively, which also constituted empires, left abundant material in the way of pictorial books and oral histories as well as the remains of impressive cities. Others, such as those of China, the Indus Valley, the Middle East, North Africa and around the Mediterranean have left a mass of written material for historians to use in reconstructing the past. Historical reconstructions are necessarily partial both in the sense of being incomplete as well as reflecting the subjective concerns of whoever is undertaking the task. Nonetheless, there is a significant body of knowledge about past communities, states and empires produced through the collective efforts of many different historians and archaeologists, and this allows one to make some reasonably accurate generalizations about the past in terms of notable historical events, political structures and elements of political thought.

Although the main focus here is on states, the historical legacies of empires are important too. These are large-scale political entities made up of a number of smaller political communities with a central controlling power and usually held together by force. The ancient empires constituted a kind of international system in themselves, although very different from the current international state system, underpinned as it is by the theory of sovereign equality among the constituent members. In contrast, empires both ancient and modern were characterized largely by relations of domination and subordination. Among the earliest known empires were those situated around the river systems of the Tigris, Euphrates and the Nile. Their geographical location suggests a certain correlation between the kind of environment required for successful agriculture and the establishment of settled political communities with extensive networks of relations between them. This broad region gave rise to the Sumerian, Egyptian, Babylonian, Assyrian and Persian empires which flourished between about 4000 BC and 400 BC. The methods of domination used by the controlling powers of these empires varied from direct control over the smaller, subject communities to more indirect methods which allowed a measure of autonomy to local groups as long as regular tributes were forthcoming (Stern, 2000, p. 57).

Moving further to the east, the ancient kingdoms of the Indus Valley together comprised a broad civilizational entity, with the Hindu religion and Sanskrit language providing some basic cultural cohesion over much of the region. This, however, scarcely prevented warfare between the kingdoms and other political units which included oligarchies and republics. To the extent that empires existed in the region, the best known was established in the north in 300 BC. Although it lasted less than a century, its reputation was assured largely because one of its leading figures, Kautilya, produced a highly sophisticated text on statecraft, the *Arthasastra*, which had a profound influence for many centuries. The literal meaning of *Arthasastra* is the study of the ways and means of acquiring territory, keeping it, and reaping prosperity from it (see, generally, Spellman, 1964). In some ways it rivals Machiavelli's writings on statecraft for its grim depiction of the struggle for domination.

One of the most extensive and durable of all empires was the Chinese. Despite covering an enormous territory ranging over some difficult terrain, the Chinese empire lasted from the time of the founding of the Shang dynasty in the eighteenth century BC until the early twentieth century, although there was a substantial interlude during which time it disintegrated into a number of warring states. An interesting point of comparison between the Chinese and ancient Greek world view is that both regarded themselves as inherently superior to the peoples that surrounded them – they were 'civilized', whereas virtually all others were barbarians and therefore vastly inferior. Notions of 'Chineseness' and 'Greekness' were therefore ways of understanding oneself, and one's position in the world, in relation to others. Self-regarding notions of what it is to be civilized aside, the adjectives with which empires such as 'Chinese' have been described are indeed applied regularly to a whole 'civilization'. In this sense, the Chinese empire, along with others, are generally regarded as constituting large-scale *cultural* complexes as much as a political ones. However, empires as such are not the only entities associated with civilization. Islam, for example, has been regarded as constituting a 'civilization' quite separately from the Ottoman and Moghul empires.

Today we also talk readily of 'Western' civilization as comprising a broad but nonetheless coherent category. The historical sociologist Michael Mann asserts that modern Western civilization (which includes Russia) is the most powerful of human societies to date. This, he says, has arisen not from any law of historical necessity but from mere contingency – 'it just happened that way' (Mann, 1986, p. 31). Although not based on an extant empire, 'Western civilization' may be seen as having arisen out of several historical empires including the amorphous medieval entity known as Christendom as well as the modern European empires that were not disbanded until the mid- to late twentieth century. Its deeper historical origins, however, are actually Eastern. As Mann points out, its roots are to be found in the ancient Near East with a trail of development that moves gradually west and north through Anatolia, Asia Minor and the Levant to the eastern Mediterranean, eventually entering Western Europe and ending in its furthermost state, Great Britain, in the eighteenth century (ibid., p. 31). A common, and much narrower view, however, names the ancient Greek and Roman empires as the cradle of Western civilization.

The British Empire, the largest and most powerful, practically encircled the globe, thereby giving rise to the expression: 'The sun never sets on the British Empire.' Considering the extent of the empire, and the fact that it once included the original colonies of what is now the US, it is scarcely surprising that British (or more particularly English) culture was spread around the world. This is manifest in the fact that English prevails as the major international language. It is not only required for many practical international purposes (for example, all international aircraft pilots and air-traffic controllers must use English), it is also used by many regional organizations that lie completely outside English-speaking areas.

The Association of South-East Asian Nations (ASEAN), for example, uses English as its official medium of communication.

Given the political and economic domination of the countries comprising 'the West' today, a comparison with the notion of empire is tempting. I discuss this further, together with current ideas about 'civilizations', when I come to consider the role of culture in world politics. For the moment, it should be noted that, although there are significant problems with the way in which the term has been deployed in the analysis of world politics, 'civilization' does serve as a useful shorthand expression in describing the kind of broad cultural complexes associated with the ancient social and political systems discussed above. Having said that, it is equally important to note that these cultural complexes nonetheless contained any number of ambiguities, contradictions and other conflicting tendencies within them. And the same certainly applies to civilizational entities today.

Political community and human nature

There is no single concept of human nature. Some political theories assume that humans possess a natural disposition to act or behave in one way, while others take a very different view of what humans are by nature inclined to do. Still others reject the notion that there is any such thing as a universal or essential human nature at all, arguing that all human behaviour is shaped by local factors to do with culture and circumstance and will therefore differ according to time and place. However, the position taken on whether or not there is such a thing as human nature and, if so, what exactly constitutes this nature, is central to theories of political community and their relations with each other.

Even if one rejects the notion of a universal human nature it is nonetheless difficult to reject out of hand the argument that humans are very much inclined to live within communities rather than as isolated individuals having little or no contact with others. So, even if one were inclined to adopt a cultural relativist position in opposition to the universalist position on human nature, one would first have to concede the *universal* existence of cultural communities within which particular human behavioural patterns are formed. And so we come to the claim of Aristotle (384–322 BC) that the human is, by nature, a political animal. Because this term is so widely misused and misunderstood as referring to a nature which is cunning and conniving, it is worth setting out precisely what Aristotle meant, for he had something very different in mind.

Aristotle's philosophy of politics, like that of other philosophers of his time – including his teacher, Plato (427–347 BC) – centred very largely on the political community. Although well aware of the existence of other forms in other places, the particular type of community that Aristotle analysed – and idealized – was his own, the Greek city-state or *polis*. By the fifth century BC, the city-states around the Hellenic region numbered about 1500, of which Athens and Sparta are the best known. Apart from their political philosophies, these two states are remembered for engaging in a lengthy war recorded in detail by Thucydides (*c.* 460–400 BC) in his *History of the Peloponnesian War.* Thucydides' text has sometimes been claimed as a classic in the realist tradition for its reporting of the cold-blooded reasoning of the Athenians in justifying the slaughter of the entire adult male population of Melos, a city that had refused to submit to Athenian domination. As noted below, the realist tradition contains an explicit theory of human nature. It is not, however, related directly to Aristotle's.

The word *polis* itself gives a clue to what Aristotle meant by 'political animal', for the words 'political' and 'polity' (another term for political community) are derived from the same root as *polis*. Thus when Aristotle used the term *zōon politikon* he meant literally that the human being was by nature a 'creature of the *polis*', made for living in a political community. Put another way, the political community was the *natural* habitat of humans, and it was this characteristic that distinguished them from gods and beasts alike. The polity was also conceived as a moral or ethical association within which the good life could be pursued (Barker, 1959, pp. 14–15). Thus it was only within the political community that any sort of genuinely human, civilized life was possible. But more than this, for Aristotle and most of his contemporaries, the conditions for the highest form of civilized existence, the good life, could be found only within the Greek *polis*. Other communities, namely those inhabited by barbarians, occupied more lowly positions in a hierarchy of political communities.

Aristotle showed clear ethnocentric prejudices in his writings, common among Greeks of the time – and still common enough today. Although he had a keen interest in comparative studies, he paid little attention to the methods of government in non-Greek states even though knowledge of them was readily available. Ironically, just as Aristotle was working out his philosophy of the state, with the *polis* at the pinnacle of state forms, the Greek city-state had just reached the stage of terminal decline, and nothing similar in the way of political community was to emerge again until the Italian city-states came to prominence in the Middle Ages (Russell, [1946], 1979, p. 196). These observations reinforce two important lessons. First, that no state form is permanent, however solid – and desirable – it may seem at any given time. And second, that ethnocentrism, while certainly an extremely common disposition (perhaps even part of human nature), carries with it a handicap – and that is the inability to discern and appreciate what other ways of life have to offer.

The issue of human nature goes beyond the question of whether or not people are creatures of community. It is clear, for one thing, that there are many different types of community and that the internal political arrangements for each are infinitely variable. Human nature might therefore incline people to live in political communities, but does it dictate any particular kind? The short answer is no. Not only are there different types of polities, there are different types of governments as well. To explain further, the Greek city-state was a particular kind of state but that did not mean that all of them had the same type of government or form of rule. Among the city-states that Aristotle studied, he distinguished a number of different forms of rule, from democracy to oligarchy, aristocracy, tyranny and monarchy. It is also worth noting here that the condition of a polity which had no ruler or body exercising authority within the state was described as anarchy, a word derived from ancient Greek that means literally 'no ruler'. Anarchy does not mean chaos, although many political theorists have argued that without a structure of enforceable rules within a polity there can be no proper order, and without order, no justice. As explored below, the concept of anarchy is central to traditional approaches to international relations and world order.

Themes concerning human nature and rule within a political community continued to pervade political thought in Europe from the time of the Greek philosophers onwards. Some important developments came with the emergence of Christian political philosophy and bore the influence of Greek thought. St Augustine of Hippo (354–430) believed that the necessity for the state, with an apparatus of political authority, had come about due to the fallen nature of humankind. Whereas God had originally created humans with a completely innocent nature, the 'fall from grace' (occasioned by Eve and Adam eating the apple from the tree of knowledge of good and evil in the Garden of Eden) meant that human nature became indelibly marked by this act of original sin. Not only was human nature therefore in need of redemption, it also required containment within a state and subordination to the rule of a coercive political authority, without which all the worst tendencies of human nature would be given free rein. A very different account of human nature and the state was provided by St Thomas Aquinas (1224–74). Aquinas endorsed the Aristotelian view of the state as an entirely natural entity – even in the state of innocence. The state was not required just for the purpose of containing wicked inclinations as Augustine believed, and political rule was not simply seen as a coercive instrument made necessary by such inclinations, but in a positive light as a natural mechanism for ensuring the common good (Morrall, 2/1960, pp. 68–80). Aquinas thus endorsed Aristotle's view of human nature and the purpose and function of the state, declaring that the human was indeed a social and political animal and had been so from the moment of creation.

Philosophies associated with other traditions of thought also contain explicit theories of human nature linked to political theories concerning the state. It is assumed in most systems of thought that the natural human habitat is a community living under a system of rules and norms. Hindu political thought, for example, places the human within a fixed framework of cosmic order of which community is an integral part. Harmony is maintained as long as people adhere to their prescribed roles and duties which are ordained at birth according to their caste position. But humans, with their capacity for independent thought and action, may be inclined to deviate from their given place and so coercive authority is needed to keep them in check and prevent disorder. Interestingly, Hindu thought contains a vision of a golden age, similar to the conditions within the Garden of Eden, when people were so well attuned to their own specific *dharma* (roles and duties) that coercion through government was unnecessary. But, like Eden, it did not last and other human characteristics such as greed and self-interest led to corruption and, eventually, the necessity for coercive rule. Shades of Augustine are clearly evident here.

As with Christian thought, the development of Islamic thought was influenced by Greek philosophers, especially Plato and Aristotle. The necessity of human association in a political community is generally endorsed, as is the requirement of coercive rule to maintain order, peace and justice. Among the philosophers of early Islam, ibn Khaldūn (1332–1406) sets out an account of the development of organized human community and various types of political authority. These are based on the assumption that although humans are by nature rapacious and co-operate only with difficulty, they cannot survive as isolated individuals. Like many other philosophers in the Islamic and early Christian traditions, Khaldūn endorses an authoritarian and hierarchical form of rule as necessary for order (see, generally, von Grunebaum, 1953). So too does the Chinese tradition of Confucianism, even though most versions of Confucian teaching see benevolence as the principal virtue embedded in human nature. But benevolence does not emerge unaided. Rather, it must be nurtured via an appropriate education. The Confucian scholar Mencius (372–289 BC) developed the notion that appetite was an even more fundamental aspect of human nature. This trait represented a fundamental danger to social and political order and it could only be properly controlled by strong rule under the authority of a monarchical figure together with a council of Confucian advisers (see, generally, Lau, 1970; Lau, 1979). In this respect, Mencius' views paralleled those of Thomas Hobbes some eighteen hundred years later, which I consider shortly in the context of the rise of modernity.

So far I have examined views from different sources on the relationship between the state and human nature. One more needs to be mentioned here, and this derives from a tradition of thought that was developed by philosophers spanning the Greek and Roman worlds (including parts of the Middle East), and which rejects key aspects of thought about the *polis* and the extent to which it encompassed all aspects of human existence. For Aristotle, as already mentioned, life was bound up almost completely within the city-state. And although he could certainly contemplate the idea of universals, these did not extend to provide a basic equality for all people. For both Plato and Aristotle, it may have been ethically wrong, for example, to enslave Greeks, but not so others. However, from the time of Alexander the Great, who did much to modify the distinction between Greeks and barbarians, through to the end of the Roman Empire, there was a shift in thinking which contemplated, at least in theory, a community of humankind – a *cosmopolis* – in which all were regarded as intrinsically equal. This idea is associated most specifically with Stoic philosophy, which held that, *by nature*, all human beings are equal. The doctrines associated with natural law, natural rights and natural equality that appeared in Western European thought from the sixteenth century represented the revival of key aspects of Stoic thought. And these are the basis on which theories of universal human rights, so prominent in contemporary normative international theory, were eventually developed.

Much of Europe, along with parts of North Africa and the Middle East, had been subject to the imperial ambitions of Rome. But the Roman Empire, like all others in history, could not be sustained permanently as an international system held together by force and it broke down under the impact of a combination of factors. The legacies were many. One was the idea of a world society under a single civilizational umbrella, and this accorded with Stoic philosophy too. Of course, Rome had not taken over the entire world but the basic conception was there. This idea, moreover, was entirely compatible with the universal, monotheistic religions of Christianity and Islam which sprang from a similar source, both having roots in Judaism.

The universalist idea was also to become a central element in modernity, especially as this was manifest in the eighteenth-century intellectual movement known as the Enlightenment. In the meantime, Christianity had been adopted as the official religion in the final stages of the Roman Empire. But the Christian world then split into two parts, one Eastern, based in Constantinople (now Istanbul), and the other Western, based in Rome. Christianity of course had an overwhelming impact in Europe and gave rise, among other things, to the idea of 'Christendom'. This gave an appearance of unity across the otherwise chaotic political landscape of the medieval period. With the coming of modernity, however, not only Europe but the entire world came to be organized on a much more systematic and integrated basis.

The rise of modernity

It has been said that the first glimmerings of the modern as opposed to the medieval outlook began in Italy with the Renaissance period from the mid-thirteenth century through to the sixteenth. This epoch, most commonly associated with a great flourishing of art and architecture and names such as Michelangelo and Leonardo da Vinci, derived its artistic inspiration and aesthetic expression from the rediscovery of classical civilization. But it was also a time when some began to liberate their thinking from the confines imposed by the medieval church. Intellectuals now drew in part on the authority of 'the ancients' (of Greek and Roman civilization) instead of exclusively from the church (Russell, [1946], 1979, p. 483). Other ideas and inventions that influenced change at this time, however, were imported from China and Arabia and even some of the influences from Greece and Rome were transmitted via Islamic influences (see Stern, 2000, p. 72).

This was also the period in which the Italian city-states rose to prominence. Many were organized on republican principles inspired by ancient examples of participatory government. In turn, these ideas fed into a form of civic humanism the classical character of which was expressed in the idea that 'man is the measure of all things'. A related development was the growth of secularism and, although this by no means amounted to a rejection of religion, it encouraged at least the conceptual separation of church and state. The political map of Europe revealed many small autonomous and semi-autonomous polities and overlapping jurisdictions. The multiplicity of authorities meant that conflict was frequent and insecurity became the order of the day. Richard W. Mansbach (1997, p. 45) compares these general conditions with those of some contemporary 'failed states' (e.g. Somalia). While the Church remained more or less united, it provided an overarching legal and moral order for

Christian Europe. But much was to change with the Protestant Reformation which saw the emergence of a much more distinctive secular political realm, something which is a defining feature of modernity in general and the modern state in particular.

The best known political thinker of the period was Niccolò Machiavelli (1469–1527) of Florence. His handbook of practical advice to rulers, otherwise known as *The Prince*, has ensured a place for him in the history of IR theory as well as political theory more generally, and, like Thucydides, he has been claimed by many of those in the realist tradition for providing much 'bleak wisdom' about politics and war (Howard, 1983, p. 1). In terms of statecraft, Machiavelli focused broadly on how principalities (states) may be acquired and maintained as well as on how they are lost. He is widely interpreted as repudiating morality in favour of necessity and invoking *raison d'état* (reason of state) in choosing strategies for survival. Goodness in a ruler, though admirable in some respects, is almost certainly a political weakness and it is far better to be as cunning as a fox when practical circumstances dictate. This is much more like the 'political animal' to which Aristotle's conception has so often been mistakenly applied. But there is more to Machiavelli than this. George H. Sabine (1948, p. 293) argues that Machiavelli was not indifferent to issues of morality and that while he may have made recommendations on the use of immoral means to achieve certain ends, he never doubted that moral corruption made good government impossible.

Modernity is also associated with the development of science. Bertrand Russell ([1946], 1979, p. 512) goes so far as to say that: 'Almost everything that distinguishes the modern world from earlier centuries is attributable to science, which achieved the most spectacular triumphs in the seventeenth century.' Scientific discoveries also provided the basis for key aspects of Enlightenment philosophy. As a complex philosophical movement, the Enlightenment cannot be defined in any simple way, but several related strands of thought stand out as characteristic. First, Enlightenment thinkers generally subscribed to an evolutionary notion of historical progress. This applied not only in science, but also to society which could be continually improved by the application of human reason to political and social problems. Second, they called for the emancipation of human reason from the fear and superstition instilled by conventional religious institutions and practices. This was assisted by the availability of scientific explanations for previously inexplicable and mysterious phenomena. And third, the Enlightenment promoted universalist notions which underscored emerging concepts not only of the universal capacity of all humans for rational thought, but also of their inherent equality in terms of rights.

The sovereign state and state system

In the meantime, during the Reformation, warfare in Europe spread as struggles for political and moral supremacy between Catholics and Protestants emerged. The most notable war was prosecuted by the Catholic Habsburg dynasty which controlled territory ranging across significant parts of Western and Eastern Europe. Known as the Thirty Years War, it ended in 1648 with the Peace of Westphalia. Although the principles established at Westphalia with respect to the authority of rulers to determine the religious affiliations of their subjects were similar to those agreed earlier with the Peace of Augsburg in 1555, for students of IR Westphalia is usually taken as the beginning of the modern period proper, and it is certainly to this time that the concrete beginnings of the modern sovereign state and state system are conventionally traced (but for an alternative view see Reus-Smit, 1999, p. 88).

The Thirty Years War had ended not only with the defeat of the Habsburgs but, most importantly, with a recognition that Catholics and Protestants had to find a means of peaceful coexistence. Since the Reformation, the idea of Christian unity under a single religious authority was clearly untenable. The Westphalian settlement was underpinned by emerging ideas about international law which could transcend religious differences and therefore be applied universally (that is, to Catholic and Protestant states alike). The foremost thinker along these lines was the Dutch jurist Hugo Grotius (1583–1645) whose seminal (*Laws of War and Peace*) confronted directly the problem of conflicting moralities and the need for toleration as well as setting out minimum standards for conduct.

The key principle to emerge and take practical effect in achieving this desirable state of affairs was sovereignty. In terms of international relations, the emphasis was on the external dimension of the state. Enclosing states within a 'hard shell' of sovereignty – with the shell corresponding to the territorial borders – was meant to guarantee non-interference in the internal governmental arrangements or any other domestic affairs of a state. The theory was admirably simple in conception. Rulers within states could do more or less what they liked, follow whatever religious principles they chose and govern according to whichever form of rule they preferred – republicanism for the republicans, monarchy for the monarchists, Catholicism for the Catholics and so on. The hard shell of sovereignty would guarantee the autonomy and independence of each state to determine its own affairs, regardless of the approval or disapproval of external actors, no matter how big or small it was in terms of size and regardless of its relative power and capacity. This 'juridical' sovereignty remains a basic principle of international law today and is why the Kingdom of Tonga enjoys equal sovereign status with the United States of America. But Richard Falk (1999, p. 21) argues that the formulation of a world of sovereign states as reflected in the Westphalian vision never actually described political reality. Rather, it needs to be understood as a world order project (in terms of a world to be created rather than one that exists), and a mystifying ideology that provides a juridical mask for *in*equality.

Political behaviour within states raises another dimension of sovereignty that is equally important, the matter of 'internal' sovereignty: this concerns how, and by whom, legitimate political power is exercised *within* the state. This is an issue around which a great deal of political theorizing had always taken place but in post-Renaissance Europe it took on added importance. One of the earlier theorists, Jean Bodin (1539–96), was concerned principally with how peace and stability could best be secured and concluded that only a sovereign monarch could do the job effectively. Thomas Hobbes (1588–1679), however, is the theorist of sovereignty best known to students of IR. He followed Bodin in endorsing the sovereign monarch as most likely to secure order within the state, although he allowed that collective bodies such as a parliament might do as second best. But it was his depiction of the state of nature, against which order must be secured, that has captured the imagination of IR theorists (see, generally, King [1974], 1999). And here again arises the question of human nature *vis-à-vis* the state of nature.

In the Hobbesian state of nature there are no rules, no government, no leaders, no community. All are equal, and equally free from coercive rule. In this sense the state of nature is clearly anarchic. But it is no anarchic utopia. Nor does it represent a state of innocence as in the Garden of Eden. Rather, the state of nature is highly dangerous and totally lacking in justice or morality. Fear and insecurity are the dominant feelings and the main motivating force behind human action in such an environment is individual self-preservation. Domination is the only means of achieving this, but since all are therefore driven to dominate, the inevitable result is an incessant war of all against all. It is impossible for people to be at peace with one another, and so life in the state of nature is, in Hobbes's famous words, 'solitary, poor, nasty, brutish and short'.

The only means of finding genuine peace and security is through forming a community by means of individuals contracting to live under a single political authority – a sovereign – who has absolute power and therefore the necessary capacity to enforce order and obedience. The only fundamental right that people retained was that of self-preservation, since it was for this purpose that they had submitted to the sovereign authority in the first place. In summary, Hobbes believed that political communities are artificial constructs devised to alleviate the miserable conditions that are our 'natural' lot. As for relations between states, these are the same as for individuals in the state of nature. Since there is no overarching sovereign in the international sphere, states are condemned to exist in a realm of perpetual anarchy. Justice and morality are absent and survival is achieved only through domination and the pursuit of pure self-interest. This, in bare outline, is taken to be a classic realist view of international relations.

The 'peaceful coexistence' strategy described above simply required acknowledgement of the sovereign status of other states and a commitment to non-interference. Peace and security, justice and morality *within* states were the business of the ruler. This remains a key feature of realist thought. Europe after the Peace of Westphalia, however, remained subject to warfare as struggles for political control over territory – and the resources that go with it – continued apace. And within states, Catholics persecuted Protestants, Protestants persecuted Catholics, witches were persecuted in general, torture was a fairly standard part of many legal systems, and the idea of universal human rights was a long way off. Indeed, the formulation of the principles of state sovereignty, which effectively relativized an entire range of political and moral considerations within states, were clearly opposed to any kind of universalism – except that of the principle of state sovereignty itself. Even then, the 'universe' as such was confined to Europe and the rules of the 'international' state system only applied there. Non-interference in the affairs of political communities outside Europe was another thing altogether, which brings me to the modern colonial empires.

The modern colonial empires

The Americas had already been 'discovered' in the late fifteenth century with large-scale European settlement following soon after. Aided by rapid developments in technology – including shipping technology as well as weaponry – the scramble for further possessions in distant lands led to Europeans eventually spanning out over the entire globe. Britain, France, Spain, Portugal and the Netherlands were the principal colonizers in the earlier period. They were joined by Germany, Belgium and Italy in the nineteenth and twentieth centuries. The US, Russia and Japan also participated in the colonial enterprise during the later phase while the Ottoman Empire lasted until the early twentieth century. The tentacles of the European empires, however, were the longest and strongest and eventually reached right around the globe.

Not all colonies were acquired for their potential riches. Some, such as most of the colonies in Australia, originally provided a dumping ground for human refuse. Nor were colonies always imposed on local people. At least one British colony, Fiji, was established at the invitation of indigenous political elites. Other forces behind colonialism were to do with 'civilization' and the 'white man's burden'. For many Europeans, both Catholic and Protestant, civilizing meant conversion to Christianity, and it was a duty owed to God to support the missionary cause.

But for other Europeans, the spread of 'civilization' served only to corrupt the innocence of 'savage' peoples in other parts of the world. These sentiments were associated with philosophers such as Jean-Jacques Rousseau (1712–78) and, more generally, with the Romantic movement in Europe which represented a reaction against the corruption of European society thought to be brought about by modernity. The latter was characterized, in particular, by industrialization as well as aspects of the philosophy of the Enlightenment. Although Rousseau is often regarded as one of the Enlightenment's *philosophes,* his ideas represented a view of human nature that considered so-called 'progress' and 'civilization' to be responsible for the corruption of an originally good and innocent human nature. Moreover, the political and social institutions of modern society amounted to a kind of prison, leading Rousseau to declare famously that 'man is born free, yet everywhere he is in chains'.

The empires held by Western Europeans were not the only ones. I have mentioned the Chinese, Moghul and Ottoman empires as other examples. Each of these constituted an extended economic and political system. They also spread their cultural practices far and wide. Islam, for example, is found not only in the vicinity of its birthplace in the Middle East, but was carried through the Ottoman and Moghul empires to parts of Eastern Europe as well as Central and South Asia and, eventually, to South-East and East Asia. Indonesia is now the most populous Islamic country in the world. Japan also had an empire, albeit a smaller and more localized one. Today, 'global' culture is seen largely as 'Western' culture writ large, but significant aspects of what we often take for granted as Western, including technologies and artefacts, do not have their origins in 'the West' at all: gunpowder was a Chinese invention; the 'Arabic' system of numerals is so called with good reason (although the Arabs acquired them from India in the first place); tattooing is a Polynesian art; the Walkman (and Discman) are Japanese in origin; and when you next bite into a croissant, you might remember that it represents the symbol of Islam – the crescent. From the earliest times, all of the colonial empires, whether Egyptian, Greek, Roman, Moghul, Chinese, European, Ottoman, Russian or Japanese, have been implicated in the spread of economic links as well as cultural practices and artefacts and therefore, to a greater or lesser extent, in the broad processes of 'globalization'.

Nationalism and the nation-state

No account of the state would be complete without reference to nationalism, arguably one of the most powerful ideologies of the modern period. It developed as a direct result of two crucial factors in the seventeenth and eighteenth centuries. The first was the emergence of the sovereign state itself, as described above, through which nationalism acquired its central rationale – the ideal of national self-determination within an autonomous, independent, bounded political community that existed alongside, but separate from, other such communities. The second factor was the French Revolution (1789), which occurred against the backdrop of Enlightenment philosophy, especially its emancipatory ideals, and a pervasive mood of social and political discontent with the existing order. The French Revolution was the most memorable event in a period of history that saw off the *ancien régime* by effectively declaring that the mass of ordinary people, peasants, farmers, merchants and artisans alike, were no longer subjects of a monarch, but citizens of a state. Sovereignty was now to reside, not in the person of the king, but in the people of France as a whole – in the collectivity known as *la nation*. This was, obviously, an important moment in the modern history of democracy as well as nationalism (see Cassells, 1996, esp. pp. 18–19). But in its future development, nationalism was also to ally itself with creeds that were anything but democratic. It is also interesting to note that the word 'terrorism' has its origins in the French Revolution. Although democratic ideals served as an inspiration, the practices of the French state following the revolution abandoned these, and tactics of terror were used without compunction to deal with political enemies.

In the wake of the revolution in France, the nascent ideology of nationalism became infused with some of the ideals of German Romanticism. These included an image of the people or *Volk* as comprising an historic community bound together by an unbroken chain of tradition reaching back into the mists of time. This was manifest in shared language, poetry, songs and dance. Each nation's set of collective traditions was unique and therefore each nation was unique in itself. Individuals were submerged in the community and drew their identity almost exclusively from it. Some of these ideas were developed in detail by Johann Herder (1744–1803) who is generally known as the founding figure of cultural history. His concept of culture also provided the basis for the later development of cultural anthropology, which in turn gave rise to the doctrines of cultural and ethical relativism. This anthropological concept of culture, and the relativist doctrines derived from it, underscore important aspects of normative international theory today, especially as it is manifest in communitarian thought (see Lawson, 1998b).

Nationalism became strongly influenced by Herder's culturalist approach to community. Although Herder himself did not link his theories to political doctrines revolving around the state, and in fact opposed aspects of centralized political authority, later developments saw the fusion of culturalist ideals and political nationalism. This became manifest in its most repugnant form in the ideology of national socialism in the twentieth century. Herder, however, would have been horrified at the brutal uses to which Hitler and the Nazis put his theories of culture, history and the *Volk*.

CONCLUSION

This discussion of states in history has provided an overview of both the practical development of state forms as well as the political ideas underscoring them. The rise of the modern state in Europe, with its sovereign and national attributes, obviously represents only one phase in the history of states. Nonetheless, it is this form that has become 'globalized' and that now provides the universal standard for virtually all states. A persistent current of thought has revolved around the subject of human nature. In turn, the various views on human nature have generated different ideas about the purpose of the state, especially as to how power and authority should be exercised, and by whom. The Hobbesian theory, in particular, has been taken to characterize relations between states in a very profound way. This characterization occurred as the discipline of IR developed in the twentieth century. It was not, however, the only outlook influencing thinking on the subject of states and the state system. As explored below, idealism, in one form or another, has also had a very significant impact on both the theory and practice of international relations.

3

The 'Short' Twentieth Century

At the close of the twentieth century it was widely remarked that it had been the bloodiest one-hundred-year period in the history of the human species. In addition to the Holocaust, between them Stalin's rule of the USSR, Mao's 'Great Leap Forward', Pol Pot's gruesome regime in Cambodia and other genocidal tragedies in places like Rwanda and Guatemala claimed millions of lives. The increasing sophistication of technologies also transformed warfare into a phenomenon quite different from that of previous centuries. This became known as 'total war', meaning that it was not just armies that engaged each other directly – entire nations and all their resources were mobilized to contribute to the war effort. And although 'world' war may be just a little exaggerated in terms of actual participation in the wars of 1914–18 and 1939–45, it nonetheless conveys the enormous scale of these episodes.

The Cold War of 1945–89 also drew in most countries around the globe in one way or another, and was therefore in effect another world war. And although it did not involve major 'hot' warfare between the main protagonists, many of the smaller wars fought around the world during this period, and which claimed hundreds of thousands of lives over four decades or so, were directly related to superpower rivalry. Moreover, it was during the Cold War that the annihilation of humanity became a real possibility. All three episodes in world politics had a profound effect on the discipline of IR. And indeed, it was as a direct result of the First World War that IR was actually founded as an academic subject in its own right. In this chapter I discuss these developments largely within the time frame provided by these three 'world wars' which together comprise the 'short' twentieth century from 1914 to 1989.*

The first conflagration

Although the idea of the sovereign nation-state, as well as a 'society' of such states coexisting under a set of common principles, had arisen more than two centuries earlier, Europe had continued to experience a fair degree of political turmoil. The Napoleonic Wars of 1795–1815 in particular had threatened to upset the emergent state system. Nonetheless, this period was followed by a relatively tranquil stretch and Europe experienced no large-scale warfare for almost a hundred years. One important factor accounting for this happy state of affairs was the balance of power achieved between the 'Great Powers' that had defeated Napoleon. Britain, France, Prussia and Austria together conducted what is known as the 'Concert of Europe'. This was based on balance of power diplomacy, and was manifest in an *ad hoc* series of multilateral conferences designed to forestall trouble. But despite some successes, major trouble was brewing. The processes of state formation in Europe had been ongoing throughout the period. Germany was not unified as a single nation-state until the 1870s and, when it was, it comprised by far the biggest state in Europe, overshadowing all its neighbours in terms of both territory and population size. Germany's economic and industrial strength was also considerable. And when Germany began a project of expansion in Europe as well as imperial outreach in the quest for enhanced trading and market opportunities as well as status, there was considerable resistance among Europe's established powers, all fearful of Germany's potential for domination.

These developments, together with the instability caused by the decline of the Austro-Hungarian, Ottoman and Tsarist Russian empires and the accompanying rise of nationalism in parts of Eastern and Central Europe, combined to produce the conditions under which a single political incident – the assassination of the heir to the Austro-Hungarian Empire, the Archduke Ferdinand, by a Serb nationalist in Sarajevo – could spark off by far the worst conflict witnessed on the European continent to that time. And it was soon to draw in many other parts of the world as well. By the end of the 'Great War', as it became known, around

---

* The idea of the 'short' twentieth century is attributable to Eric Hobsbawm (1994), although his dates differ slightly since he ends his short century in 1991 when the USSR dissolved whereas the present discussion takes the collapse of the Cold War in 1989 as the end point.

nine million people had died – of these about eight million were military personnel and one million were civilians. Moreover, although Europe and other parts of the world had suffered warfare before, the devastation in terms of loss of life and destruction of property, the enormous scale and unprecedented geographic spread of this particular conflict, not to mention the sheer pointlessness, was an experience on a different plane altogether.

The liberal search for peace and security

One vital question asked on many occasions since that fatal day in Sarajevo is this: how did a single incident spark off such a disastrous episode in world history? Of course there is no simple answer to this question, just as there is usually no simple explanation for any significant event or set of events in world politics. Nor does the study of such episodes seem to have helped our powers of prediction, or prevention, very much. Even so, the search for answers and solutions to these questions and problems in the immediate aftermath of the horrors of the war became a serious concern in both practical and intellectual terms. It was in this context that the academic study of IR as a discipline became formally established. Before then, the subject matter was certainly studied, but often as part of history, law and political theory rather than within a dedicated discipline. Brian Schmidt (1998, p. 231) notes that intellectual work from the 1880s onwards provided a vital basis for the discourses that surrounded the subject in the inter-war years and in 1900, obviously well before the events of 1914–18, a book entitled *World Politics* by Paul Reinsch was published, indicating that IR's field of study had already taken shape.

The first university professorship in the formally established discipline was the Woodrow Wilson Chair of International Politics established at University College Wales, Aberystwyth, in 1919. It was endowed by David Davies, a Welsh philanthropist and MP, who hoped that a better understanding of politics in the international sphere would promote lasting peace and security. The chair was named after the US president in recognition of his dedication to the attempt to find a lasting solution to the problem of deadly conflict, for which he was also awarded the Nobel Peace Prize in the same year. Wilson (1856–1924), a former professor of political science himself, had brought the US into the war to 'make the world safe for democracy'. He was a committed proponent of the idea that democracies do not go to war against each other. If all Europe had been governed under liberal democratic regimes, the war simply would not have happened. By extension, the further liberal democracy as a form of government is spread throughout the world, the more likely it is that the world as a whole will become more peaceful. Interestingly, a similar idea characterized Marxist thought, although in Marxist theory it was the rise and spread of socialism that was to put an end to conflict.

Wilson's views about the democratic peace were not entirely novel. The 'democratic peace thesis' goes back to the Enlightenment philosopher Immanuel Kant (1724–1804), whose scheme for 'perpetual peace' was based on the belief that citizens of a democratic (or republican) state characteristically evince much greater reluctance to engage in violent conflict, primarily because they are reluctant to risk their own lives. It is not that ordinary people in non-democratic states are greater risk-takers. The simple fact is that the decision to go to war is not theirs to take, nor does their influence in terms of 'public opinion' necessarily count for anything. It is within the sole power of the ruler to declare war. Kant's view that people are constrained by their own rational interests to avoid war wherever possible resonated with that of other liberal thinkers such as Jeremy Bentham who, along with John Locke (1632–1704) and Adam Smith (1723–90), are among the most important theorists contributing to the liberal tradition of political thought in general, and 'liberal internationalism' in particular.

Although there are many different strands of liberal thought, a theme throughout many liberal writings, past and present, is a more optimistic view of the possibilities for peaceful relations among humans. For some liberals this derives from a more positive assessment of human nature, at least to the extent that they can learn from their mistakes, but also confidence in the capacity of individual humans to choose *rational* courses of action in politics, as in other fields such as economics (see Sargent, 1999, p. 107). Such courses of rational action may well be self-interested – which is hardly surprising given that self-interested behaviour is, for liberals, a key aspect of human nature. But the general effect of rationally chosen, self-regarding courses of action by individuals tends, happily, to lead to better outcomes for all, or at least for the majority. And over the course of time progress towards a better state of existence can be achieved.

But later liberals perceived that this was not going to come about unaided. Human rationality must be consciously applied to the construction of international institutions designed specifically to overcome the negative effects of anarchy and to contain tendencies to war. It was this thinking that underpinned developments in the immediate aftermath of the First World War. Wilson was instrumental in establishing the League of Nations, the first real attempt at setting up an international organization dedicated to preserving international peace and security. Thus the first experiment in 'global governance' was born. Wilson's basic ideas, and hopes, were set out in his famous 'fourteen points' addressed to a joint session of the US Congress on 8 January 1918; this address was to form the basis of the peace in November 1918.

The first thirteen points concerned a variety of pressing issues arising from the war. These included: the necessity for transparency in any international covenants; the freedom of navigation of international waters; the lowering of barriers to trade; the reduction of national armaments; an 'impartial adjustment' of colonial claims; independent determination by Russia of internal political development; restoration of French territory, including Alsace-Lorraine (taken by Prussia in 1871); and readjustment of Italy's borders along points of nationality as well as determination of the borders in the Balkans on similar principles. The Turkish part of the Ottoman Empire was to become a sovereign entity, but development of other parts was to be autonomous. Poland was to be granted independent sovereign statehood. The fourteenth point in the 'program of the world's peace' proposed the formation of a general association of nations 'under specific covenants for the purpose of affording mutual guarantees of political and economic independence and territorial integrity to great and small states alike'.

Wilson's 'points' were adopted as the basis for the post-war peace settlement. The Covenant for the League of Nations was officially drawn up in 1919 by the victors – Britain, France, Italy, the US and Japan – but Wilson was its principal architect. The US Senate, however, could not come to an agreement on the terms, and in March 1920 they declined to sign the Treaty of Versailles, which would have made them members of the League. This was only one of many problems that beset the nascent organization. It was designed to function as a collective security organization – replacing the secret alliances that had formerly been entered into between states and which were seen as one of the main problems in maintaining international peace. The idea of collective security was underscored by the principle that an attack on one member of the League would be met by unified action by all, although such action was to be voluntary. However, most of the member states had other agendas to pursue, and lacked commitment to the League's basic principles. It failed to function as it was meant to, and it certainly failed to prevent a second world war. The problems of the League are generally seen as bound up at least partly in the terms of the Treaty of Versailles, which laid the blame for the First World War squarely at the feet of the defeated Germans who were required to pay dearly for their aggression. In retrospect, however, perhaps the price was too high, and not just for Germany.

Another important liberal theme that emerged at this time was reflected in the idea of self-determination. Here again both Kant and Wilson had something in common. Kant's idea of the 'categorical imperative' entailed a notion of personal moral behaviour linked directly to the concept of individual autonomy or self-determination. Here one of the basic messages of the Enlightenment should be recalled – that humans should free their minds from fear and superstition, using their natural capacity for reason to determine their own goals. Kant urged that people have courage to use their own reason for this purpose – self-determination in this sense, he said, *was* enlightenment. The subsequent career of the self-determination concept, however, saw it linked specifically to groups rather than individuals and, in the end, to 'nations'. It was also transformed into a 'right'. The right to self-determination further strengthened the legitimacy of the nation-state idea, and what is called the normative nationalist principle – a state for each nation, a nation for each state (Gellner, 1986, p. 125). Another point to note is that these ideas had been developed largely with European problems in mind. They were not applied to colonized peoples outside Europe whose quest for national self-determination was not to be realized for several more decades.

Liberal approaches to IR, often referred to collectively as 'idealism' or sometimes 'utopianism' (especially by its critics), reached a high point in the inter-war years. The first holder of the Woodrow Wilson Chair, Sir Alfred E. Zimmern, was an enthusiastic, if overly optimistic, proponent of various internationalist causes and enterprises, including the League of Nations. He was also a founding member of the Royal Institute of International Affairs. And whatever other criticisms they may have attracted later, Zimmern and other liberals of his time, including Wilson and Davies, have been recognized widely as the founders of IR as an academic discipline.

From 'peace in our time' to the return of total war

The Treaty of Versailles had failed to resolve a number of Europe's political problems, and had in fact exacerbated others, especially with respect to the new states in Eastern Europe, created in an attempt to apply the principle of self-determination. Although the architects of the peace feared Germany's ability to rise again, the creation of the new Eastern Europe simply surrounded it with weak and vulnerable states. These turned out to be easy pickings when Germany rebuilt its military strength. However, there was another motive behind the support for self-determination, and that was the wish to create a number of 'buffer' states between Western Europe and the new communist empire centred in Moscow, the Union of Soviet Socialist Republics (USSR) which was widely regarded as a threat – and not without reason. Communism at that time had its own version of internationalism, but one that was obviously completely at odds with the liberals. Whereas liberalism provided the foundation for modern capitalist economics, communism was committed to its overthrow by means of a worldwide revolution, one stage of which was the establishment of the Socialist International – otherwise known as Comintern – which was active from 1919 to 1943 and which aimed to build an international network of communist parties dedicated to the cause.

Among the international economic problems generated by the First World War was the overall weakening of the global economy, although for a time this was masked by the strength of the US economy. America had come out of the war as the new economic powerhouse. It was by far the largest producer, exporter, lender and financer. Problems with currency exchanges, labour markets and falling commodity prices were among a number of factors leading to the 'Great Crash' of the New York Stock Exchange in November 1929. While globalization involves a ripple effect of economic events around the world, the Great Crash caused a tidal wave. In both economic and social terms, the global impact was devastating. By 1932 industrial production in many countries had halved and world trade had shrunk by a third (Kennedy, 1988, pp. 364–5). And in Europe, a negative impact on political as well as military developments was inevitable.

Up until the end of the 1920s, however, it seemed that a new and peaceful era of international politics really had dawned. Only two countries, Paraguay and Bolivia, were in armed conflict, and a number of important international agreements had been reached. One was the Kellogg-Briand Pact, engineered by the French and US Foreign Ministers (after which it was named). All who subscribed to the pact agreed not to use war as a way of settling disputes; when it came into force in July 1929, sixty-five countries had signed up. Other specific agreements made under the Locarno Treaties were specifically designed to mediate relations in Europe, especially between France and Germany which remained strained in the aftermath of the First World War. Thus Germany, under the stewardship of competent and shrewd politicians, gradually achieved a 'reconciliation' with its former enemies in Europe. It even joined the League of Nations. The Locarno Treaties, however, left open many possibilities for Germany, not least in terms of eastward expansion to create *Lebensraum* (living space) for the Germans of the emergent Third Reich. France was also to regret vacating the Rhineland, while an even deeper cause of regret must have been the failure by all to prevent Germany's covert rearmament. By the time Hitler was appointed Chancellor in 1933, Germany's military strength was already considerable. Neville Chamberlain signed the infamous Munich agreement with Hitler in

1938. It purportedly symbolized a mutual desire for 'peace in our time', but it soon became recognized in the UK and elsewhere as an ineffectual act of appeasement of an aggressive and militaristic Germany that was now armed to the teeth.

My focus has been very largely on Europe, with some attention to the US, but developments in other parts of the world are important too, and none more so than the rise of Japan as an Asia-Pacific power. From the late 1860s, during the period known as the Meiji Restoration, the internal feudal-like order and policy of isolationism was abandoned in favour of rapid Western-style industrialization and regional outreach. Japan grew enormously in strength and influence, both economically and militarily. It also developed imperialist ambitions and made advances in Korea, Taiwan and China. This brought Japan into armed conflict with Russia in 1904–5 in the Chinese region of Manchuria. The war ended in defeat for the Russians which, as has often been remarked, was also the first time that a non-Western state had triumphed over a European power.

Japan's momentum strengthened throughout the next few decades. Domination of the immediate East Asian region was enhanced by the virtual collapse of China towards the end of the nineteenth century. Japan took advantage of the vacuum and in 1933, the same year that Hitler won a landslide election in Germany, Japan established a puppet state in Manchuria. Japan had been a member of the League of Nations virtually from the start, but in the period leading up to the occupation of Manchuria, it had become increasingly dissatisfied with aspects of the Versailles settlement. Some actors within Japan remained committed to internationalism despite this, but others of a more aggressive, militaristic persuasion gained the upper hand. As in Germany and Italy, the effects of the Depression enhanced the influence of right-wing extremists resulting in the emergence of a particularly virile form of nationalism (see Carruthers, 2/2001, p. 64). Japan was now well along the path to confrontation with its former allies and trading partners in the West.

It was Germany, however, that finally triggered the descent into what became the Second World War with the invasion of Poland in September 1939. Over the next six years, more than fifty million people were killed as a direct result of the war. This time more than twice as many civilians died as did soldiers. And of those at least six million were deliberately murdered, on the grounds of their religious/ethnic identity as Jews or Gypsies, in that act of genocide, the Holocaust. The notion of a crime against 'humanity' was born and some kind of symbolic justice was extracted at the Nuremburg trials. As for the academic study of IR, as well as state practice and diplomacy, liberal idealism was now to take a back seat to a much more 'realistic' approach to world politics.

Realism: Telling it how it is

By the end of the 1930s it appeared glaringly obvious to some that idealist principles were out of touch with reality. Such views were held by the distinguished fourth occupant of the Woodrow Wilson Chair at Aberystwyth, Edward Hallett Carr (whose tenure there was from 1936 to 1947). Carr was a disillusioned liberal whose critique of 'utopianism' in his famous text *The Twenty Years' Crisis* ([1939], 1948) has since been claimed as a classic in the realist tradition. There is no doubting that he considered the peace settlement after the First World War a fiasco. One of the main defects in the thought processes that had gone into the settlement, and into subsequent actions (or non-actions), had been complete neglect of the power factor in politics which, he believed, operated effectively along the lines of a law of nature.

Carr also considered that the study of international politics during the inter-war period had been infected by 'primitive utopianism'. He recognized that the study of politics – international or domestic – has a strong normative dimension, since it is the study 'not only of what is, but what ought to be' ([1939], 1948, p. 5). But he went on to argue that, in their devotion to visionary projects, investigators often paid too little attention to the facts, and it was only when such projects broke down under the weight of their own idealistic but ill-founded assumptions that many investigators at last grasped the importance of analysis, after which 'the study, emerging from its infantile and utopian period, will establish its claim to be regarded as a science' (ibid., p. 5).

For Carr, Machiavelli was the first significant political theorist in the realist tradition, and he quotes him on the 'revolt against utopianism', which occurred in Machiavelli's own time, to reinforce his point about the present:

> It being my intention to write a thing which shall be more useful to him that apprehends it, it appears to me more appropriate to follow up the real truth of a matter than the imagination of it; for many have pictured republics and principalities which in fact have never been seen and known, because how one lives is so far distant from how one ought to live that he who neglects what is done for what ought to be done sooner effects his ruin than his preservation. (Machiavelli, quoted in Carr [1939], 1948, p. 63)

Given his attack on utopianism and the emphasis on the importance of power politics, it is not surprising that Carr has often been cast as realist. But he was also at pains to point out that when realism is attacked with its own weapons, it is just as likely to be lacking the cold objectivity claimed for it by its proponents as any other mode of thought (Carr [1939], 1948, p. 89). His assessment of both modes of thought therefore led him to conclude that sound political thinking must be based on elements of both utopia and reality: 'When utopianism has become a hollow and intolerable sham, which serves merely as a disguise for the interests of the privileged, the realist performs an indispensable service in unmasking it. But pure realism can offer nothing but a naked struggle for power which makes any kind of international society impossible' (ibid., p. 93).

So far I have considered the development of IR almost exclusively in the context of developments in the UK. This is because it was there that most of the influential intellectual activity of the inter-war years took place, although the influence of American idealists such as Wilson was obviously very important as well. Europe was also the epicentre of international politics at the time. In the aftermath of the Second World War and with the onset of the Cold War, however, the discipline of IR, especially in its realist mode, developed very rapidly in the US. The outstanding figure in the early years of the American realist tradition is undoubtedly Hans J. Morgenthau, who contributed another classic text to the discipline, *Politics among Nations: The Struggle for Power and Peace,* first published in 1948. The opening lines of his first chapter leave no doubt as to his central theme:

> International politics, like all politics, is a struggle for power. Whatever the ultimate aims of international politics, power is always the immediate aim. Statesmen and peoples may ultimately seek freedom, security, prosperity, or power itself. They may define their goals in terms of a religious, philosophic, economic, or social ideal. They may hope that this ideal will materialize through its own inner force, through divine intervention, or through the natural development of human affairs. But whenever they strive to realize their goal by means of international politics, they do so by striving for power. (Morgenthau, 1948, p. 13)

Morgenthau finds the basic drive for power, as in all social forces, to be rooted in human nature (ibid., p. 4). But there is more to his account than such a crude reductionist position might at first glance indicate. In considering more complex aspects of social and political behaviour, Morgenthau places a significant emphasis on the restraints on power that operate to moderate the Hobbesian state of nature in the international sphere. A world in which 'power not only reigns supreme, but without rival, engenders that revolt against power, which is as universal as the aspiration for power itself' (ibid., p. 169). Here enter the concepts of reason, morality and justice. Morgenthau, however, concedes little to idealism in examining these. Rather, he says that those who seek power will, in order to stave off the revolt against them, simply employ normative ideologies to conceal their true aims (ibid.). In this respect he is very much in tune with Carr, for whom he had much admiration.

As with all other writers and thinkers discussed so far, there is a great deal more to Morgenthau's outlook on international politics than can even be alluded to here, and the motive forces surrounding the drive to power form only one aspect of his monumental work. He has much more to say about issues such as security and the character of the international system. With respect to the latter, however, it was left to a subsequent generation of realist scholars to take up the notion of structure and make it the basis of their analysis.

Neoliberalism, neorealism and Marxism

Most systems of thought respond to challenges. If they did not, then they would simply fade away. In the 1970s and 1980s both liberalism and realism were reconfigured to meet new challenges, mostly from each other but also from Marxism. The first to fight back was liberalism which, as noted above, was treated quite savagely by its critics at the onset of the Second World War and immediately after. The school of neoliberal thought that arose to meet the realist challenge is known generally as 'pluralism'. It rejected the singular simplicities of the realist approach. For example, whereas realism took the state as the only really significant actor in international politics, and a unitary one at that (meaning that it acted as a single, coherent, undifferentiated unit), the new school of liberal thought emphasized a plurality of actors in the international system. An important precursor to the rise of this mode of thought was the 'interdependence' model of international relations promoted by Robert O. Keohane and Joseph S. Nye (1977) which, as the term suggests, highlights the linkages between actors in the international system and their sensitivity and vulnerability to the effects of each other's decisions and actions rather than their independence and self-sufficiency (see also Nye, 3/2000, p. 179).

It was also in this environment that peace studies or peace research became effectively institutionalized. Since realism had become the dominant IR paradigm after the Second World War, peace research, with its strong normative orientation, filled an important gap in studies of world politics. This normative basis gave peace studies a strongly idealist character, and there were clear links with liberalism in IR. As a field of study, however, peace research was more strongly interdisciplinary. In fact the difference between IR and peace research lies at least partly in the fact that IR was institutionalized as an academic discipline in its own right, whereas peace research became institutionalized, not merely as a sub-discipline of IR, but as a multidisciplinary enterprise with a distinct focus on conflict and violence.

With respect to the plurality of actors in the international system, while it may be true that the UN and regional organizations such as the EU, ASEAN and the African Union (formerly Organization for African Unity (OAU)) remain state-based and state-sponsored, other important actors include a huge range of important multinational corporations (MNCs), the International Monetary Fund (IMF) and the World Bank, each of which enjoys a significant measure of autonomy. These are in addition to international non-government organizations (NGOs) such as the Red Cross, Red Crescent, Médecins sans Frontières, Amnesty International, the International Olympic Committee and a whole host of sporting, professional and religious associations which are by no means merely agencies of states. Moreover, most of them operate or function between the domestic and the international sphere, thus transcending the state and in some sense erasing its boundaries.

The NGOs and other organizations described above are often taken as constituting an 'international civil society'. This term, which has great currency today, carries with it a generally positive connotation. However, not all such organizations have admirable, let alone legitimate, purposes. There is also a significant range of non-state organizations operating along illegitimate, criminal lines (although they may be covertly state-sponsored). These include organizations set up for the purpose of money laundering, the smuggling of drugs, arms and people, and for terrorism. All of these non-state organizations, whether legitimate or illegitimate, 'good' or 'bad', exercise a measure of power and influence in world affairs and must therefore be considered along with states as international actors in their own right. This kind of claim is now commonplace in discussions about globalization.

To summarize briefly, the contribution that earlier pluralists made in the 1970s was to open up the domain of IR to a much broader range of considerations by demonstrating the extent to which both non-state actors and processes in the international sphere played a significant part in world affairs. In this respect, the pluralist contribution constituted a challenge for realism precisely because there was no place within the latter to account for these important non-state factors. According to the pluralists, then, realism was not 'telling it how it is' in full, but providing only a very partial account of 'reality'.

The pluralist response to realism in turn precipitated a counter-response. The key figure in the realist renewal in the 1970s was the US scholar Kenneth Waltz. His key strategy for meeting the pluralist challenge was set out in his highly influential *Theory of International Politics* (1979). But an earlier work, *Man, the State and War* (Waltz [1954], 1959), laid the essential bases on which the neorealist paradigm (otherwise known as structural realism) rests. In this, he identifies three 'images' of politics, each of which translates into a level of analysis – individuals, states and the international state system. More specifically, the causes of war in the first image relate to human nature and behaviour – from selfishness, misdirected aggressiveness and stupidity (ibid., p. 16). According to the second image, the internal organization of states is the key factor in understanding war and peace (ibid., p. 81). The third image takes the condition of states in the international system, namely the condition of anarchy, as defining the essential structure within which war is bound to occur (ibid., p. 159). This is the image or sphere with which IR scholars must be almost exclusively concerned.

In addressing questions of balance of power and self-help in this environment, Waltz explains how game theory helps to illustrate the problems, as well as how power must be understood in terms of capabilities.

> States . . . do not enjoy even an imperfect guarantee of their security unless they set out to provide it for themselves. If security is something the state wants, then this desire, together with the conditions in which all states exist, imposes certain requirements on a foreign policy that pretends to be rational. . . . The clue to the limitations imposed by the condition of anarchy among states is contained in the maxim: "Everybody's strategy depends on everyone else' " . . . The implication of game theory [is that] the freedom of choice of any one state is limited by the actions of all others. . . . If some states seek an advantage over others, they combine; if other states want to counteract this advantage, they in turn combine. If the advantage sought is measured in terms of power to destroy or damage another state, then the threatened state refrains from the effort to increase its strength only at the risk of its survival. Pursuing a balance-of-power policy is still a matter of choice, but the alternatives are those of probable suicide on the one hand and the active playing of the power-politics game on the other. . . . The cardinal rule of the game is often taken to be: Do whatever you must in order to win it. If some states act on this rule, or are expected to act on it, other states must adjust their strategies accordingly. The opportunity and at times the necessity of using force distinguishes the balance of power in international politics from the balances of power that form

inside a state. In both cases we can define power, following Hobbes, as the capacity to produce an intended effect. . . . In international politics there is no authority effectively able to prohibit the use of force. The balance of power among states becomes a balance of all the capabilities, including physical force, that states choose to use in pursuing their goals. (Waltz [1954], 1959, pp. 201–5).

Waltz is much more precise than Morgenthau about what he is willing to include in the scope of 'international theory', and by limiting the scope of the theoretical field to a narrow focus on the structure of the international system and the overwhelmingly predominant role of states within it, he bracketed off many of the issues that liberal pluralists included. The distinct levels of analysis used also had the effect of rigidly separating the domestic from the international. In summary, Waltz's work emphasizes the extent to which the inescapable condition of anarchy provokes the logically necessary self-regarding behaviour of states essential to survival in an environment where, ultimately, it is every state for itself. These arguments were mounted against both liberalism and Marxism.

For Waltz and other neorealists, the dangers in this environment are many, not least because an effort by one state to provide for its own security (such as enhancing the national arsenal) is more than likely to provoke insecurity in another state, which may then respond by an arms build-up of its own and therefore become even more dangerous. This is known as the 'security dilemma'. It also illustrates the key neorealist concept of the balance of power as each state adjusts to the behaviour of other states that are likely to affect them. In turn, this reveals the extent to which structure – in this case the structure of the anarchical environment of international politics – determines the conditions in which actors or agents (states, governments and so on) must play their roles. In other words, structure trumps agency in the neorealist paradigm.

Before moving on to consider the Marxist contribution, there is another important body of work that developed from the 1970s, but which does not fit neatly within either the realist or liberal moulds described above, although it has often been regarded as a milder version of realism. This is the 'English School' (although one of its most prominent figures, Hedley Bull, was Australian). One of its most significant contributions concerns the concept of 'international society'. The editors of *The Expansion of International Society* (Bull and Watson, 1984, p. 1) explain that an international society may be regional or global, and it may involve a group of states, such as modern sovereign states or independent political communities such as those that existed in pre-modern periods. It comprises more than a mere system in which each state simply calculates and responds to the behaviour of others. An international society is a group of states that has established 'by dialogue and consent common rules and institutions for the conduct of their relations, and recognize their common interest in maintaining these arrangements'.

International society theorists have generally taken states as the primary units of analysis rather than any sub-state or non-state form of organization, and also tend to reject universalist ideas about 'humanity' (Brown, 1997, p. 52), embracing instead a form of relativism. There has also been a strong focus on the importance of power politics. But this apparently realist emphasis is moderated in the sense that the notion of international society entails a strong element of shared norms. It is this normative dimension that ameliorates, although by no means banishes, anarchy in the international sphere. Anarchy in international society is nonetheless rendered orderly, thus promoting the conditions for peace and security as well as the preconditions for justice. The normative foundations for international society were laid out in Hedley Bull's major work, *The Anarchical Society* (1977). Some of the important ideas about international society are considered in more detail in chapter 6 in the context of global governance and world order, but are mentioned here as an antidote to the widespread view that this period in the development of IR consisted almost exclusively of debates between neoliberals and neorealists on the other side of the Atlantic.

Another significant contribution to debates in IR which provided a direct challenge to both realism and liberalism came from Marxist viewpoints. These took a number of forms, some of them contradictory. At base, however, all Marxist variants have had a strong normative concern with the exploitative nature of capitalism and its impact on the social world of humanity at large. One of the most prominent schools of Marxist thought in the twentieth century was world-system theory, articulated first by Lenin in 1917 in a work on imperialism. By identifying a particular structural characteristic of the developing world economy in terms of uneven development, he found a 'core-periphery' bifurcation of the world later taken up by dependency theorists concerned with the study of international political economy (IPE); this was further developed in the 1970s by Immanuel Wallerstein, who added a category of semi-periphery as well. A key feature of world-system theory is the transfer of wealth and resources from peripheral countries to those in the core, meaning that the rich get richer while the poor get poorer (Hobden and Wyn Jones, 2/2001, pp. 207–8). An interesting aspect of Wallerstein's approach, as noted by Richard Little (1995, p. 80), is that it never defined the world in terms of strategic bipolarity during the Cold War period. Rather, the 'core-periphery' bifurcation referred to the relative economic strength of rich countries (i.e. those in North America and Europe as well as Japan), which form the core of the world economy, and poorer ones on the periphery, with the Soviet Union occupying the semi-periphery.

Important contributions to the study of IPE and world order have also been made by scholars working within a tradition of critical thought attributable to the Italian Marxist thinker Antonio Gramsci (1891–1937), who developed a concept of hegemony that dealt with power in a way quite different from realist approaches, although he also drew on aspects of Machiavelli's thought. In brief, Gramsci proposed that although power was often exercised through blatantly oppressive means, including the use or threat of crude force, it is most effectively exercised where those subject to it actually consent to it. This consent is obtained through the hegemony of a ruling class who are in a position to set the standards for political and moral behaviour. Over time, these standards become part of the normal or natural landscape of a society and may then go quite unquestioned. These ideas have been taken up and developed by critical theorists in the contemporary period interested in the wider problem of world order. I return to some of these points later. For the moment it should be noted that while Marxist theories of IR were critical of both liberals and realists, these were in turn obviously critical of Marxist ideas. For one thing, non-Marxist theorists, especially those subscribing to basic realist principles, pointed out that Marxists generally failed to take account of the crucial role of geopolitics and warfare in the development of human society, a view that seemed to be strongly supported by the great power struggles in the post-war period (Linklater, 2/2001, p. 144).

As shown in the discussion of the ideas of Waltz and other realists, the overriding structure of the international system was, of course, provided by the Cold War. More specifically, the structure was bipolar: the two main power blocs, headed by the USSR and the US, dominated the international system. In this aspect, as in others, the Cold War had a significant development on the discipline as a whole when it finally came to an end in 1989. I therefore backtrack a little and consider other developments in the context of world politics in this period.

The changing structure of world politics, 1945–1989

Even though the Great War of 1914–18 had devastated the continent, Europe nonetheless remained at the centre of world politics in the inter-war years. This was largely unaffected by the economic dominance of the US, which was more concerned with its influence in Latin America than elsewhere for much of the time. Despite the currency of the doctrine of self-determination, European powers had also retained control of their empires. Some, however, had changed hands during the war. Former German possessions in the Pacific, for example, had been lost in the early stages of the war and they were later handed over to other countries to administer under mandates awarded by the League of Nations. But while this may have dented Germany's prestige, it hardly affected Germany's ability to rebuild. Indeed, small distant colonies were usually more of an economic liability than anything else and their possession conferred not much more than status. After the Second World War the international atmosphere changed markedly as the 'winds of change' gathered momentum: between 1945 and 1980 the number of independent countries around the world more than doubled.

Ironically, the creation of new sovereign states via decolonization effectively completed the globalization of the European state system. Some former European colonies had already become independent states in the nineteenth century and the early twentieth. These were the settler colonies once held by Spain and Portugal in Latin America as well as the former British colonies of Australia, New Zealand, South Africa and Canada. In all of these, waves of immigrants from the European home-lands had virtually swamped indigenous populations. Now, the colonized people of the continents of Africa and Asia as well as most of the islands, or island groups, in the Caribbean and the Pacific and Indian oceans sought the same sovereign status. Even in places that had never been colonized, such as the kingdoms of Thailand and Tonga, the European sovereign state form had nonetheless been adopted. The United Nations, launched at a conference in San Francisco in 1945, made states the basis of its membership. And as former colonial states gained independence, most of them joined this international club of states. From an original membership of 51, the UN had grown to 159 by 1984. After 1989 membership increased again, due largely to the collapse of the former USSR, and by 2000 it stood at 189.

At much the same time that the Cold War was brewing, the UN was founded as an organization committed to constructing and maintaining a new and peaceful world order. And although alternative courses of world history can only ever be speculative, it is possible that without the UN the Cold War may well have turned into a major hot one. Also, given the short- as well as long-term destructive capacity of nuclear weapons, it would have been a world war in the fullest sense of the word. Even though a major worldwide war did not actually break out, its effects were nonetheless felt globally. And despite the establishment of a 'non-aligned' movement to which a considerable number of Third World countries belonged, most countries did in fact support one or other of the two power blocs. Many of the smaller wars fought in the Third World were obviously related directly to Cold War dynamics. These included the Korean War and the Vietnam War as well as civil wars fought in the name of either communism or anti-communism. The legacies of many of these wars are still with us, the most obvious being the case of Afghanistan. So although the Cold War may be over, its deadly effects are likely to live on well into the future.

But what caused the Cold War in the first place? Given that the USSR and the US had been allied against the Axis powers in the Second World War, it may have been expected that this common cause would have laid the basis for more positive relations in the future. But the demise of a mutual enemy left the two most powerful countries in the world, with their deeply opposed ideologies as well as a new-found willingness to project their power, confronting each other on a world stage largely vacated by the European powers. The division of Europe after the war, and the way in which it was managed, reflected the entrenched positions of each of the two new superpowers. Agreements reached at the Yalta conference in February 1945 between Churchill, Roosevelt and Stalin, and a further conference at Potsdam six months later, envisaged a post-war settlement of Europe that included the effective partition of Germany into four occupation zones with a central council in Berlin, as well as the holding of democratic elections in the states of Eastern Europe. Since no actual peace treaty was drawn up when the war ended, these agreements stood as the only effective accord. However, the principles agreed to at these conferences were not upheld and the politics of post-war settlement in Europe became a source of major tensions, effectively precipitating the Cold War. Attempts to apportion 'blame' to one side or the other for leading the world into the Cold War have proved futile. Rather, a consensus emerged, at least among scholars, that it was 'the result of a complex pattern of actions and interactions in which domestic politics, leaders' personalities, misperceptions and misunderstandings all played a part in producing the tangle of relations which later became known as the cold war' (Bowker, 1997, p. 245).

Crucial to early US policy towards the USSR was the 'containment' of the USSR's ambitions within the boundaries set out at Yalta. The influential US diplomat George Kennan first put the basic policy idea forward in 1947. Its scope was initially quite limited, but was subsequently given much wider application by the overarching 'Truman doctrine', which sought to provide active protection and support for 'free peoples' threatened by subversion within or by pressures without. Initially, aid was approved only for Turkey, Greece and Iran in the early post-war years, as these were seen to be especially vulnerable to the USSR's ambitions. However, the Truman doctrine soon became the basis of US support for a variety of repressive right-wing regimes around the world whose only credentials for claiming to be freedom-loving were their virulent anti-communism. This led to covert as well as overt US intervention in such places as Chile and Vietnam, to which Kennan himself was deeply opposed.

A more successful post-war policy devised by the US was the Marshall Plan. Officially known as the European Recovery Programme, it supplied grants and credits to the countries of Western Europe totalling some $13.2 billion. Between 1948 and 1952, the plan's achievements had exceeded original expectations, with European industrial production rising to 35 per cent and agricultural production to 10 per cent above pre-war levels. US aid to Western Europe had enormous benefits for the US economy too, as it stimulated significant markets for its exports. The recovery programme was further assisted by a new international monetary system, which included the establishment of the International Monetary Fund (IMF) and the International Bank for Reconstruction and Development (IBRD – more popularly known as the World Bank), planned at a meeting of forty-four allied nations at the Bretton Woods resort in New Hampshire in 1944 (Keylor, 1996, p. 264). A major benefit in the eyes of the US, and one of the original purposes of the Marshall Plan, however, was to create a strong Western Europe which could withstand any threat from the USSR. Three years later, the General Agreement on Tariffs and Trade (GATT) was instituted in order to stimulate a system of free international trade.

Another important development in the defence of Western Europe was the establishment of the North Atlantic Treaty Organization (NATO) in April 1949. This was effected in the wake of the Berlin crisis. The city of Berlin was geographically in the heart of the USSR's occupation zone, but had itself been divided into different occupation zones. When the USSR blockaded all land routes from the west into the city, the US and the UK instituted an airlift of vital supplies into their sectors. The USSR subsequently dismantled the blockade rather than attempt an escalation of the conflict but the tensions caused by this incident, among others, prompted the establishment of a military alliance with the aim of deterring further aggressive behaviour. In turn, the USSR sponsored the Warsaw Pact, although it took until May 1955 for this to come about and it did little to change existing security relations in the east which were, in any case, controlled completely from Moscow – as demonstrated by the invasion of Czechoslovakia by Warsaw Pact troops in 1968 (Bowker, 1997, pp. 86–7).

On the other side of the world, the Second World War ended a little later, and with a devastating display of the latest development in weaponry. While Berlin had fallen to the Allies by May 1945, the war in Japan did not end until August when the US airforce dropped atomic bombs on the Japanese cities of Nagasaki and Hiroshima. This action has been seen as both the closing shot of the Second World War as well as an opening shot of the Cold War, as it was designed not only to convince the Japanese that further resistance was pointless, but to provide a demonstration of superior strength to the Soviets, and so dissuade them from pursuing any further claims in the Pacific, let alone any role in the post-war administration of Japan. Unlike Germany, then, the subsequent political rehabilitation of Japan was left completely in US hands.

The Cold War in Asia was to take on an additional dimension with the victory of Mao Zedong's Chinese Communist Party over the nationalist, and pro-Western, forces led by Chiang Kai-Shek in 1949. The latter retreated to Taiwan while Mao consolidated his hold on mainland China. The largest country in the world was now under communist control. But it was never to enjoy close ties with Moscow. Although Chinese communism failed to attract such epithets as 'the evil empire', in the way that Soviet communism did, thousands of US lives were nonetheless lost fighting wars in China's sphere of influence. The first on the Korean peninsula claimed nearly 28,000 US lives while the second in Vietnam resulted in over 58,000 deaths. While the war in Korea was something of a stalemate, Vietnam was clearly a defeat. This long and bitter episode in which so many young American soldiers died (along with conscripts from allies such as Australia and New Zealand), apparently for nothing, created what later became known as the 'Vietnam syndrome'. In brief, this denoted a US policy position limiting the circumstances in which US troops might be committed to fighting conflicts abroad. The position was somewhat modified by the Gulf War of 1991 and since 11 September 2001 the syndrome as such seems to have been overcome, as evidenced by the almost complete lack of hesitation in sending American troops abroad to prosecute the 'war against terrorism'.

Tragic though these wars have been for all concerned, they did not approach the scale of previous world wars. Nor did they involve the weapons of mass destruction (nuclear, chemical or biological) now available. However, if a third world war of a 'hot' variety had broken out and weapons of mass destruction deployed, you would not now, in all likelihood, be sitting reading this book. With the development of nuclear arsenals the potential for global destruction was multiplied many times over, especially since damage to the environment produced by all-out nuclear warfare could well have made the planet uninhabitable – except by cockroaches and a few other hardy plant and animal species capable of surviving intense radiation. In these circumstances, no one could possibly 'win' a nuclear war. Rather it would be a case of Mutually Assured

Destruction (MAD – surely the most appropriate acronym ever devised). Thus some have argued that the key to maintaining the 'long peace' of the Cold War was the fact that the possession of nuclear weapons by both sides effectively acted as a deterrent to both. This theory, however, has at least as many critics as supporters (see Kenny, 1985).

The end of the Cold War

The short answer to the question of why the Cold War ended is that communism collapsed in the USSR. The more complex question, of course, is, why and how did communism as a political, social and economic system disintegrate there? One could also attempt to offer a simple explanation for this: that the USSR was suffering economic collapse and communist rule could no longer sustain either the country or itself. However, economic disaster has not prevented the continuation of other communist systems – namely Cuba and North Korea. Nor has it seen off dictatorships in such countries as Iraq. Here is where agency in politics comes to the fore. And there is one 'agent' who may be seen as primarily responsible for creating the conditions under which communism could not only collapse, but do so peacefully.

There is nothing to suggest that Mikhail Gorbachev initially sought to bring about the demise of the very system that had brought him to power in March 1985 as Secretary General of the Soviet Communist Party. Indeed, he saw his reforms as being necessary for the reinvigoration of the communist system (Bowker, 1997, p. 12). But these quickly led to far-reaching changes in the whole dynamics of Soviet politics and economy. Economically, the Cold War had taken a heavy toll. The USSR had struggled to keep pace with US military developments, and the involvement in African wars as well as the débâcle in Afghanistan had strained resources to the full. The structure of the Soviet command economy was also highly inefficient. Gorbachev introduced two significant policies – glasnost (openness) and perestroika (restructuring). The first referred to a relaxation of prohibitions on freedom of expression, including a more open media and the opportunity to criticize policy. Perestroika referred to both economic reforms as well as the restructuring of the legislature and the introduction of an executive presidency, a position that Gorbachev intended to occupy in order to maintain overall command.

But he was soon to lose control of events as reformism gained a significant momentum of its own. After he declared that the Soviet Union would not intervene in the internal affairs of its East European allies, the changes in Poland, Hungary, Czechoslovakia and East Germany and elsewhere in the region gathered an even stronger impetus. These reached a climax in November 1989 with the breaching of the Berlin Wall by thousands of ordinary citizens while security forces which, in the past, would almost certainly have mowed them down with machine guns, now stood by and watched. The Bulgarian and Romanian communist governments were gone by the end of the year. While it took another two years for the Soviet Union itself to unravel, the fall of the Berlin Wall marked the effective end of the Cold War and the bipolar world order.

CONCLUSION

In the course of the 'short' twentieth century, the world was enmeshed in two grossly destructive world wars as well as a third confrontation in the form of the Cold War, in which the obliteration of the entire human race was made technically possible. It was also the period in which the discipline of IR was born. Its purpose, in the wake of the first conflagration, was to focus on the causes of war and the conditions for peace in the international sphere. This mission was taken up with renewed purpose in the wake of the second, even more ghastly experience of world war. Two distinct schools of thought on this topic emerged during the period, the first along liberal/idealist lines and the second along realist principles. Initially at least, there was no disagreement between them as to the basic purpose of the discipline, but each started from quite different assumptions about the nature of politics in the international sphere. Both also drew on long-standing traditions of thought developed over centuries of political philosophical speculation. Realists have claimed an intellectual heritage embracing some of the oldest and most enduring of the traditions, going at least as far back as the ancient Greeks. Liberal ideas as well as Marxism, on the other hand, are much more recent in origin, having their source in the rise of modernity, the Enlightenment and the industrial and economic revolutions that have taken place over the last few hundred years. Longevity, however, does not necessarily correspond to veracity, just as novelty need not lead to genuinely fresh insights. Nonetheless, all three broad traditions have made a substantial contribution to the discipline, and are likely to do so for some time to come.

4

After the Cold War

Defining moments such as the end of the Cold War invariably prompt reflections on the past and speculative thinking about what kind of world one might be moving into in the future. For those devoted to the study of world politics, it is scarcely surprising that such a momentous event should stimulate critical intellectual activity not only in relation to actual events and what they mean, but also with respect to IR itself. Although the collapse of the Cold War provided further space for developments in thinking to flourish, reflective critical thought on the discipline, its purpose, methods and agenda, had been under way well before the events of 1989. From at least the 1980s new ideas had been introduced into IR debates that departed from both realist and mainstream liberal ways of thinking as well as from orthodox Marxist analysis. By the 1990s it was rare to see an IR textbook that had nothing to say, for example, about feminism, postmodernism, environmentalism or the role of culture in world politics. Such was the intellectual ferment of the late Cold War period that one leading scholar remarked that the whole tradition of international theory was in disarray, with a three-centuries-long consensus on the proper objects of enquiry broken down under the weight of contending approaches (Holsti, 1987, p. 1).

During the period from 1989 onwards some grand ideas about world politics emerged to fill at least part of the vacuum left by the collapse of the old world order. These ranged from Francis Fukuyama's announcement of the 'end of history' to Samuel Huntington's forebodings concerning a 'clash of civilizations'. The latter, especially, has implications for post-Cold-War developments such as the incidence of deadly conflict that appears to revolve around issues of 'identity' politics, including culture, ethnicity or religion. In certain parts of the world, especially the Asia-Pacific region, the concept of culture has also featured in causal theories relating to economic growth. Ideas about culture now play a significant role in some branches of security studies as well as normative theory.

There has also been a vigorous debate about methodology and, again, although this started well before the end of the Cold War, during the post-Cold-War period with its 'new agenda' for IR greater space has been opening up for these discussions as well. One significant question that revolved almost exclusively around the end of the Cold War was this: for all the effort put into the 'scientific' study of IR in the post-war years, why had the end of the Cold War come as such a surprise? This raises the issue of methodology in IR.

Methodology and scientific IR

The development of a truly 'scientific' approach to the study of world politics had been the aim of many realist scholars during the Cold War, especially those based in the US where the 'behaviouralist' approach to social scientific enquiry was also nurtured in the post-war period. It would be a mistake to dichotomize US/non-US methodological approaches according to a corresponding positivist/non-positivist divide – something to which non-positivist scholars in the US would obviously take exception. Nonetheless, it remains the case that the positivist tradition of methodology is far stronger in the US than elsewhere (Smith, 2000, p. 375). In the UK and Australia, especially, it has always been much more marginal, with one commentator saying that it has never been more than a 'fringe movement' in the UK (Nicholson, 1996, p. 131).

Another point to note is that although adopted by many researchers subscribing to a realist approach, positivism, as a method based on a certain epistemology, is not the same as realism as a theory of international politics, although the two very often go together. In other words, one can be both a realist and a positivist, but it does not *necessarily* follow that to be a realist one must also be a positivist, or vice versa. Thinking about this issue raises, more broadly, the relationship between theory and methodology. In a recent collection of essays, which happens to take a constructivist approach to the subject matter, the editor says that 'the departures in this volume are theoretical rather than method-ological' and that the book 'neither advances nor depends on any special methodology or epistemology' (Katzenstein, ed., 1996, p. 65). This begs the question of whether theory can ever be properly separated from methodology, and whether certain theories carry with them inherent epistemological assumptions. This cannot be explored in detail here, but it is an interesting and important issue in the quest for knowledge and how it can be acquired.

A basic feature of positivism is the assumption of a 'unity of method' appropriate for both the natural and social sciences. Positivist IR set out to develop a body of theory built on objective observation and mea-surement of the 'facts' that could expose, in a properly scientific manner, the laws of action in world politics. Values and norms were considered as incapable of proper scientific evaluation. In other words, positivist approaches are generally concerned with what *is*, and not what *ought* to be. Thus, for at least the more rigid positivists, normative considerations were often bracketed off as belonging to the realm of the 'unscientific'. Even so, to engage in empirical work does not mean that one needs to adopt an approach that is blind to normative considerations, or vice versa. It has been noted, for example, that many of those engaged in peace research have been motivated by strong moral concerns while at the same time their methods have been strongly positivist. Accordingly, it has been argued that: 'Demarcation between facts and morality does not imply a lack of interest in morality either logically or empirically' (Nicholson, 1996, p. 141).

Another aspect of the positivist enterprise concerns prediction. According to the logic of scientific method, it is meant to produce theo-ries that possess not only considerable explanatory power, but at least some moderately reliable predictive capacity as well. In short, the method should allow one to see something of the future. A flaw in the positivist's crystal ball became all too evident with the sudden collapse of the Cold War and the Soviet Union – events not predicted by positivist scholars. Those deploying alternative methodologies may not have had any greater success in prediction, but then they had never claimed to be 'scientific' in this sense. In any event, IR scholars in general were possessed of no more foresight than anyone else. Indeed, the failure to predict the sea-change of the century in world politics led the foremost historian of the Cold War, John Lewis Gaddis, to launch a particularly scathing attack on the positivists, remarking that one may as well have relied on sooth-sayers, star-gazers and readers of entrails for all the good that their so-called scientific methods did (Gaddis, 1992–3, p. 18). He further suggested that the failure of this kind of IR theory arose because of a passing of methodological ships in the night. Too many in the social sciences – IR scholars among them – were seeking the holy grail of objec-tivity and certainty at a time when the natural sciences were going the other way, and recognizing the importance of factors such as indeter-minacy, chaos, contingency, chance, irregularity and unpredictability

(Gaddis, 1992–3, p. 53; see also Gaddis, 1996). World politics at the end of the twentieth century have certainly displayed these features in abundance. Perhaps one of the simplest lessons to be drawn from all this is that the future is just not all that predictable, no matter what methodological tools are deployed, and that scholars and policy-makers must always expect the unexpected. Postmodern thinkers would certainly say that disruptions, dislocations and discontinuities are more common features of social and political life than linear paths that follow a predictable trajectory.

Across the Atlantic, the English School has long offered a different approach. While accepting the need for solid empirical work to back up any claims that might be made about the political world, these scholars roundly repudiated the possibility of value-free enquiry. Instead they proposed an interpretative understanding of world politics that recognized the contingency of human action and events. Early proponents, such as Martin Wight and Hedley Bull, had incorporated in their studies a greater range of the elements at work in the global sphere, and recognized the often varied meanings that different actors may give to the same event as well as the way in which values, culture and identity shape diplomatic and political practice (Dunne, 1998, p. 187). This approach, along with a range of critical theory viewpoints, therefore accepts as a fundamental truism that facts simply do not speak for themselves. They are made to speak, often in very different ways, by different people – scholars, politicians, diplomats, bureaucrats, religious leaders and so on. And as has been noted (Woods, 1996, p. 9), different theories call upon facts in different ways and for different purposes, hence the same facts 'can tell a number of stories and lead to any one of a variety of conclusions'. This does not necessarily lead to an acceptance of relativism. It simply recognizes that facts are rarely, if ever, neutral. I return to some of these issues in the next chapter when considering various approaches to theorizing security.

Another point to note is that the range of 'facts' and issues now regarded as relevant to IR has widened considerably. With the Cold War, the USSR, bipolarity and the threat of all-out nuclear war seemingly gone, it was clearly time for a 'new agenda' as well as a fresh look at methodological approaches and theoretical approaches. As mentioned in chapter 1, this agenda now embraces a very broad range of problems and issues from AIDS and the environment to international distributive justice, religious fundamentalism and terrorism. An IR agenda that includes all these certainly seems very far removed from the field of neo-realism described in the last chapter and embraces a range of important normative concerns that go well beyond matters of inter-state war and peace.

From the end of history to a new world order

Two of the most interesting debates about the kind of world into which we might be moving emerged soon after the end of the Cold War and revolved largely around issues of ideology in world politics. The first was provoked by a claim that there was actually nothing left, ideologically speaking, to argue about – let alone fight about. This view was put forward by a US State Department official, Francis Fukuyama, even before communism was quite dead. His essay 'The End of History?' (Fukuyama, 1989) proclaimed a world in which historical progress, understood in terms of the quest for human freedom, had reached its final destination with the discovery that the promises of communism were an illusion. As with hereditary monarchy, fascism and other autocratic forms of government that had been tried from time to time, communism, the last great challenger to liberal democracy, had failed to deliver the proverbial goods.

While modern democracies were not without their practical deficiencies, and still struggled with problems of crime and social injustice, Fukuyama believed that these simply reflected the incomplete realization of modern democracy's basic principles of liberty and equality rather than any real defects in the principles themselves. Thus, while earlier forms of government had serious flaws that led to their eventual demise, liberal democracy was evidently free of fatal internal contradictions. In explaining the progressive or teleological nature of history that underscored his thesis, Fukuyama pointed to the contributions of both G. W. F. Hegel (1770–1831) and Karl Marx (1818–83). But it was Hegel's liberal vision rather than Marx's socialist dream that had clearly won out. This also meant that capitalism, as the logical economic accompaniment to liberal democracy, had also triumphed. What Fukuyama's vision did not promise, however, was a world free of the tragedy of violent conflict. After all, many places were still stuck in history and seemed likely to stay there for some time. As for everybody else in the liberal democratic world, the end of history might well mean a much more secure existence, but it may not be a very interesting or challenging time or place to exist in. Fukuyama therefore went on to suggest that one might well develop a nostalgia for the time when history existed and be driven by sheer boredom to crank it up again.

Another liberal thesis that received a boost in the early post-Cold-War period was one that owed more to the liberalism of Kant than Hegel, and this was the 'democratic peace' thesis referred to in chapter 3. With the sudden death of communism as a serious challenger to liberal democracy, and superpower hostilities at an end, there seemed to be a genuine prospect for expanding the world of democratic states, and therefore the 'zone of peace', significantly. Once again, this reflected a characteristically idealist mood of optimism about the future of world peace. But this was not based on mere wishful thinking of the kind that Carr had accused earlier liberals of in the inter-war years. Proponents of the democratic peace produced empirical evidence to demonstrate that liberal democracies *in fact*, not just in theory, do not go to war against each other.

Writing shortly after the collapse of the Soviet Empire, a leading proponent of the democratic peace thesis put the case as follows:

> The end of ideological hostility matters doubly because it represents a surrender to the force of Western values of economic and especially political freedom. To the degree that countries once ruled by autocratic systems become democratic, a striking fact about the world comes to bear on any discussion of the future of international relations: in the modern international system, democracies have almost never fought each other. This statement represents a complex phenomenon: (a) Democracies rarely fight each other (an empirical statement) because (b) they have other means of resolving conflicts between them and therefore do not need to fight each other (a prudential statement), and (c) they perceive that democracies should not fight each other (a normative statement about principles of right behaviour), which reinforces the empirical statement. By this reasoning, the more democracies there are in the world, the fewer potential adversaries . . . democracies will have and the wider the zone of peace. (Russett, 1993, p. 4)

Peace among liberal states, however, was only one aspect of the democratic peace thesis. Despite peaceful relations *between* them, students of the democratic peace thesis found that liberal democracies are nonetheless just as likely to go to war against non-democracies. In other words, they are just as prone to pursue warfare as a foreign policy strategy as are non-democracies. A brief survey of inter-state war-making by liberal democracies in the post-Cold-War period seems to bear this out. The Gulf War led by the US and various allies against Iraq, NATO's war against Serbia over Kosovo and the current 'war against terrorism' have all been prosecuted by alliances led by liberal democracies, with the US at the fore, against so-called rogue states.

It is worth noting here that the expulsion of Iraq from Kuwait by an alliance of forces under a UN Security Council mandate regenerated the general mood of euphoria that had followed the collapse of the Berlin Wall. In the absence of the old polarization in world politics, it seemed that the collective security function of the UN could at last be fulfilled. There was a very evident revival of idealist aspirations reflected in visions of a 'New World Order' based on effective international law backed up by the sanction of the UN's new-found solidarity. This basic message was delivered by President Bush to the US Congress on 6 March 1991 in the immediate aftermath of the Gulf War:

> On the night I announced Operation Desert Storm, I expressed my hope that out of the horrors of war might come new momentum for peace. . . . Twice before in this century, an entire world was convulsed by war. Twice this century, out of the horrors of war hope emerged for enduring peace. Twice before, those hopes proved to be a distant dream . . . Until now, the world we've known has been a world divided – a world of barbed wire and concrete block, conflict and cold war. Now, we can see a new world coming into view. A world in which there is the very real prospect of a new world order. . . . We've learned the hard lessons of history. The victory over Iraq was not waged as 'a war to end all wars'. Even the new world order cannot guarantee an era of perpetual peace. But enduring peace must be our mission.

But this vision was soon to be challenged by another very powerful and persuasive way of looking at the post-Cold-War order that put forward a much gloomier, and far from idealistic, vision of *dis*order emerging from so-called primordial sources of conflict.

The clash of civilizations

The idea of a 'clash of civilizations' came primarily from a prominent Harvard professor, Samuel Huntington, who took issue in particular with Francis Fukuyama's ideas. While agreeing that the old ideological battles between communism and liberal democracy were indeed over, he argued that there was little cause for complacency about other potential sources of conflict. Nor were we heading towards a world unified under a single civilizational umbrella or an order based on widespread commitment to the values of liberalism. History would continue by other means. In a highly influential article published in the summer of 1993, Huntington declared that the fundamental source of conflict in the new post-Cold-War world would be based on the great cultural divisions among humankind. While he believed that nation-states would remain the most powerful actors in world affairs, the principal conflicts would occur between nations and groups of different civilizations: 'The clash of civilizations will dominate global politics [and the] fault lines between civilizations will be the battle lines of the future . . . The next world war, if there is one, will be a war between civilizations' (Huntington, 1993, pp. 22, 39). He further declared that with the end of the Cold War, international politics was moving out of its 'Western phase', with the focal point becoming 'the interaction between the West and non-Western civilizations and among non-Western civilizations' (ibid., p. 23). Furthermore, in the politics of civilizations, 'the peoples and governments of non-Western civilizations no longer remain the objects of history as targets of Western colonialism but join the West as movers and shapers of history' (ibid.).

Huntington identified eight major civilizational groupings: Western, Confucian, Japanese, Islamic, Hindu, Slavic-Orthodox, Latin American and 'possibly' African. In explaining why civilizations were likely to clash, six basic causes were put forward. In summary, these are:

1.   Differences among civilizations are not only real; they are basic. Civilizations are differentiated by history, language, culture, tradition and, most importantly, religion. Since these differences are the products of centuries, they are not likely to disappear soon. Moreover, they are far more fundamental than differences between political ideologies, being less susceptible to change. Although differences do not inevitably lead to conflict, the evidence over the centuries shows that civilizational differences have in fact generated the most prolonged and violent conflicts.

2.   Since the world is becoming an increasingly smaller place, the interactions between people of different civilizations is increasing. Such increasing interactions have the effect of intensifying civilization consciousness as well as differences between and similarities within civilizations. This tends to invigorate differences and historical animosities, whether these are real or imagined.

3.   Economic modernization and social change throughout the world are weakening long-standing local identities as well as the nation-state as a source of identity. In many places religion has moved in to fill the vacuum, often taking the form of fundamentalist movements. These may be found within Western Christianity, Judaism, Buddhism and Hinduism as well as Islam. The revival of religion provides a basis for identity and commitment that transcends national boundaries and unites civilizations.

4.   The West has a dual role in enhancing civilizational consciousness. Since the West appears at the peak of its power, this has prompted a return-to-the-roots phenomenon among non-Western civilizations. This means that an ascendant West now confronts various non-Wests that increasingly have the desire, will and resources to shape the world in non-Western ways.

5.   Cultural differences are less mutable and hence less easily compromised and resolved than political and economic ones. In the former Soviet Union, for example, communists can become democrats, but

Russians cannot become Estonians. But even more than ethnicity, religion discriminates sharply and exclusively among people. Someone can be simultaneously half-French and half-Arab, but it is more difficult to be half-Muslim and half-Catholic.

6. Increasing economic regionalism is reinforcing civilization-consciousness. Moreover, successful regionalization may succeed only when it is rooted in a common civilization. For example, the European Community is founded on a shared European culture and Western Christianity, and the success of the North American Free Trade Agreement depends on the continuing convergence of Mexican, Canadian and American cultures. Japan presents a contrasting case. It faces many difficulties in creating a comparable economic entity in East Asia because it is a unique civilization in itself. The expansion of economic relations among Japan's East Asian neighbours, however, is proceeding apace precisely because of their shared culture.

It is clear that while conflict can, in theory, occur between any of the civilizations, Huntington pays particular attention to the possibility of conflict between the West and one or more of the other civilizational entities, arguing that the central axis of world politics in the future is likely to be a conflict between 'the West and the Rest', reflecting the 'responses of non-Western civilizations to Western power and values'. He devotes specific attention to the possibility of a 'West versus Islam' scenario, invoking images of Islam's 'bloody borders' and, in particular, 1300 years of conflict along the 'fault line' between Western and Islamic civilizations. He concludes generally that for the relevant future, there will be no universal civilization of the kind envisaged by idealists but instead a world of different civilizations, each of which will have to learn to coexist with the others if world peace is to prevail (Huntington, 1993, pp. 31–5, 41, 49).

Huntington's article has provoked numerous responses, some in agreement with his general line of argument, others highly critical of what they see as his grossly simplistic culturalist approach to world conflict. In particular, many critics have seen his work as a demonization of Islam. In the wake of the attacks in the US on 11 September 2001, however, the 'Islam versus the West' scenario appeared to come to life in the most vivid and dramatic way possible. With the identity of the hijackers being revealed very soon afterwards as Islamic ultra-fundamentalists, with highly probable links to Osama bin Laden's al-Qaida terrorist network based in Afghanistan under the protection of the Taliban regime, the 'clash of civilizations' thesis seemed to be well and truly confirmed. This was reinforced by sections of the media, with even normally circumspect and serious publications such as *The Economist* crediting Huntington for his 'cruel and sweeping' but nonetheless 'acute' observations on the nature of the Islamic threat (*The Economist*, 22–8 September 2001). As the US and its allies prepared to attack Afghanistan in its search for bin Laden, this impression was further heightened by media reports focusing on anti-US/anti-war protests led by Islamic groups around the world. But again, closer attention to the highly diverse groups that make up the universe of Islam reveals a much more complex picture. Moreover, governments within the Islamic world, including that of Pakistan – the only one that had recognized the Taliban's legitimacy – were largely supportive of the 'war on terrorism', if a little nervous of its possible consequences. Indeed, it is the governments of many of these countries that have actually had the most to fear, in political terms, from militant Islamic fundamentalist groups and which have been most vigorous in suppressing them.

While it is true that certain brands of Islamic fundamentalism are anti-Western and advocate violence as a means of achieving their political objectives, these need to be placed within a broader view not only of other ways of practising Islam, but also in a comparative framework of other forms of fundamentalism as well. As mentioned above, the latter phenomenon is scarcely restricted to Muslims. Christianity in the West has its share of fundamentalist sects as well. Moreover, many have been nurtured on American soil. And some, such as the group led by the notorious 'Reverend' Jim Jones who set up a community in Jonestown, Guyana, and which ended with the murder/suicide of over nine hundred of its members (mostly American) in November 1978, were clearly no less averse to the massacre of innocent men, women and children than those responsible for the attacks of 11 September. Also, most other Muslims and Christians would claim that neither Osama bin Laden nor Jim Jones represents any legitimate form of Islam or Christianity and that these people have done a severe injustice to both religions. The main point here is that cultural stereotypes of the kind deployed in 'clash of civilizations' scenarios are invariably superficial and misleading and serious students of IR would do well to treat them with great caution.

Ethnicity and the deadly politics of identity

Huntington's article struck a chord at the time it was written not so much because there was any real evidence that large-scale civilizational conflict was imminent, but at least partly because there were so many smaller-scale conflicts around the world that were being prosecuted under the banner of 'ethnicity', a very close relative of the culture concept. Ethnicity is in fact most commonly defined in terms of cultural elements denoting some kind of shared heritage – language, religion or history or a combination of these. Protestants in Northern Ireland, Zulus in South Africa, Tamils in Sri Lanka, First Nations in Canada, Ndebele in Zimbabwe, the Sami of northern Scandinavia, Sephardic Jews, Arya Samaji Hindus, Chechens in the Russian Federation, Roma in Eastern Europe, Hutus in Rwanda, Tajik Afghans, Christian Sudanese, Iraqi Kurds, Han Chinese, Bosnian Muslims, Indo-Fijians, Albanian Kosovars, Polynesian Hawaiians, African Americans, Vietnamese Australians and Singaporean Chinese – all these descriptors indicate an 'ethnic' identity based on one or more cultural elements.

Of the groups mentioned above as possessing an ethnic identity, some (or at least some of their members) are involved in relations of ongoing violence, and conflicts described as 'ethnic' have claimed thousands of lives in the post-Cold-War period. But it is by no means a problem unique to the present era. Ethnic conflict was a serious problem throughout the twentieth century. It was recognized by Woodrow Wilson and others involved in the League of Nations, especially with respect to Eastern Europe, and it was a key factor behind the normative theories of self-determination that were developed from that time. In the period of decolonization following the Second World War, the potential for ethnic conflict increased enormously, especially since many of the newly inde-pendent states of Africa and Asia contained very diverse ethnic groups which often spoke mutually unintelligible languages and which enjoyed anything but warm relations with each other. While some had been united in opposition to colonial rule, this did not necessarily create a bond of sufficient strength to overcome perceived conflicts of interests based on ethnic or tribal differences. Moreover, in the precarious politi-cal situations that usually followed independence, ethnic fears, sensi-tivities and insecurities were frequently used to advantage by politicians for whom identity politics seemed an obvious resource to exploit.

As the Berlin Wall fell and the former communist countries of Eastern Europe and the Soviet Union began a thorough political reconfiguration, the spectre of ethnic-based conflict once again became a prominent feature of the international political landscape. Many commentators viewed the rise of identity politics as reflecting the release of 'primordial' ethnic sentiments which had been suppressed for decades by communist authoritarian regimes. The same commentators also tended to see the break-up of the former Soviet Union as a precondition for democratiza-tion since the new, smaller and more localized political entities were assumed to be more capable of reflecting the will of 'a people' in a more substantial way. Elsewhere, political divorce was handled in varying ways. The Czech and Slovak sectors of the former Czechoslovakia enjoyed a peaceful parting of the ways. But in the former Yugoslavia it was a very different story. Slovenia and Croatia declared their independence in June 1991, with Macedonia and Bosnia-Herzegovina following soon after. The subsequent violent break-up of Yugoslavia brought, among other things, the euphemism 'ethnic cleansing' to describe the way in which some of the forces involved in the conflict sought to rid certain areas of particular ethnic groups. The tactics used in this exercise included torture, rape, abduction and mass murder.

Rather than seeing a new world order emerging along liberal idealist principles, then, many believed, with some justification, that nothing short of a brutal 'new world disorder' was a much more realistic way of seeing things. Far from ending, history was being replayed as political leaders such as the Serb arch-nationalist Slobodan Milosevic manipulated historical images of the battle of Kosovo – which occurred over six hundred years ago – to inspire feelings of strong ethnic solidarity among Serbs on the one hand and equally strong fear and loathing of non-Serbs on the other. The sheer cruelty associated with much of the violence also provided apparent evidence for the ascendancy of the wickeder side of 'human nature' in certain situations. And for those who subscribe to primordial theories of ethnic identity – which regard kinship, religion, language and so forth as having a virtually unbreakable emotional power over the members of a group – the nature of conflict not only in the Balkans but in numerous other problem areas around the world from Africa to the Pacific seemed to confirm the primacy of ethnic identity in situations of social and political uncertainty.

The apparent resurgence of ethnic conflict also focused a critical light on certain theories of modernization and development. Both liberal and Marxist scholars of the Cold War/postcolonial period generally believed that ethnic politics was an irrational curse that would pass away as rational modes of modern political organization developed. Moreover, classical liberalism as well as Marxism both promoted the primacy of economics over the attachments and motivations provided by ethnic group membership, albeit in different ways. Implicit in the assumptions of both schools of thought was the notion that ethnic identity, by virtue of its socially constructed nature, was highly amenable to transformation. This view is comparable to constructivist views of the state, discussed earlier, that regard it as a human creation subject to change according to circumstances. Once again, this draws attention to the distinction between 'culture' and 'nature' that pervades much social scientific theorizing. It also brings us to the next concern, and that is with the more general application of the culture concept to theories of world politics in the post-Cold-War period.

Culture and IR

Huntington's thesis was only one among a number of explanatory schemes revolving around the culture concept that emerged in the conceptual vacuum created by the apparent departure of ideology in the immediate post-Cold-War period. While his theoretical position was essentially a conservative one, other culturalist ideas emerged from more critical and radical quarters. These were aligned principally against the universalist, yet highly ethnocentric, thrust of many liberal ideas about the new world order. The universalist idea itself, with its roots in the Enlightenment, was seen not as a reflection of the aspirations of people all over the globe, but rather of particular values and interests within the West itself. Furthermore, it represented the projection of those values onto the rest of the world, regardless of the varied cultural and historical experiences of other places. The study of culture in world politics promised to rectify this bias and reveal the multiplicity of viewpoints, interests and alternative ways of looking at the world.

The renewed interest in culture was not confined to the sphere of world politics and the IR discipline, and it is important to note that there had already been something of a 'cultural turn' throughout the social sciences and humanities more generally. As mentioned in chapter 1, this was reflected in the rise of 'cultural studies' as well as in the extent to which scholars from other disciplines were now describing their work as 'cultural history', 'cultural politics', 'cultural geography' and so on. In development studies, too, the culture concept has come to occupy centre stage. A recent publication by the United Nations Educational, Scientific and Cultural Organization (UNESCO), the *World Culture Report 1998*, claims that culture 'is both the context for development as well as the missing factor in policies for development' (UNESCO, 1998, p. 1).

The theory and practice of multiculturalism in national societies, and its implications for such issues as immigration and citizenship, had also become a major industry by the mid- to late 1990s as well as a prominent policy issue for governments. Furthermore, from an academic point of view, the new interest in culture had the potential to cut across traditional disciplinary divisions and open up the various bounded subject areas, including IR, to important insights from other sectors of the humanities and social sciences. This certainly stood in contrast to the Cold War period when the predominance of the realist paradigm, the constraints of positivist methodology and the overwhelming concern with superpower issues left little scope for exploring such issues.

In the world of international business and finance, the culture concept was taken up with much enthusiasm in the belief that it held the ultimate explanation for phenomena such as the 'Asian miracle'. This term was used to describe the spectacular pace of economic growth in the East Asian region evident throughout the 1980s and much of the 1990s (until the financial crisis of mid-1997, which was triggered by a capital flight and the collapse of currency values). It was not merely capitalism that had proved superior as an economic system, but capitalism with a strong dash of Confucianism or, more generally, 'Asian values'. This, it was believed, had lent the Asian 'tiger economies' their distinctive form of dynamism which in turn encouraged much talk about the coming 'Pacific century'. What is especially interesting about this new-found confidence in pronouncing particularistic Asian culture and values, or more especially Confucian values, as being primarily responsible for the miracles of economic growth in the 1980s and 1990s, was that only a decade or so earlier, when growth had been sluggish and standards of living throughout the region relatively low (except for Japan), it was precisely 'Confucian' culture and values that had been blamed for backwardness and poor performance.

The more positive ideas about Asian culture and values that emerged in those two decades, however, were not confined to the economic sphere. They had broader implications for political power and legitimacy in the region. Among the more authoritarian leaders, the idea that a specific 'Asian' culture had given rise to a distinctive set of social and political values that could be contrasted with those of the West had significant appeal. In Singapore, former Prime Minister Lee Kwan Yew had devoted much energy to combating what he saw as the insidious social and political influence of 'Western values', especially those associated with individualism and political liberalism. Instead, Lee and his successor, Goh Chok Tong, sought to promote consensus politics, respect for political authority and a sense of community before self. These were essential to maintaining harmony and order. Originally put forward as specifically Confucian values, they were later transformed into a kind of 'one size fits all' set of 'Asian values' which could just as readily be attached to the major religions in the region, notably Buddhism, Hinduism and Islam. In this more flexible format, they could also be taken up by other leaders whose dominant population was not Chinese but who were nonetheless seeking a suitable weapon against 'Western values' (Lawson, 1998a, esp. p. 245). This was certainly the case with Malaysian Prime Minister Mahathir Mohamad, who became one of the foremost voices promoting 'Asian values' in South-East Asia throughout the 1990s. Interestingly, Mahathir, although a Muslim and strongly anti-Western in much of his rhetoric, is no Islamist. Indeed, the main threat to his political dominance in recent years has come from a fundamentalist Islamic party within Malaysia.

In opposing values such as individualism and political competitiveness, and labelling them as 'Western' as opposed to the allegedly 'Asian' values mentioned above, leaders such as Mahathir, Lee and Goh were effectively delegitimizing the former in an Asian context while boosting the latter. But what did this mean in specific political terms? For one thing, it indicated that political opposition to the governments in question was to be treated as a threat to the values of harmony and consensus and as a potentially disruptive and dangerous force in politics. In order to check the threat to harmony and order, expressions of political opposition therefore had to be limited. In Singapore the governing party has raised this to an art form and to this day operates the most effective constraints on opposition, not by such blatant measures as arbitrary arrest and detention under the Internal Security Act, but by the relentless surveillance and more subtle persecution of those involved with opposition groups. In Malaysia the measures have been somewhat cruder and Mahathir's major political rival, former Deputy Leader and Finance Minister, Anwar Ibrahim, is now languishing in jail after being convicted of what many observers believe to be trumped-up charges.

Elsewhere in the region, however, many countries have a much worse record on civil and political rights. Reports of atrocities in Indonesia and Myanmar (Burma), for example, have been common over the years, while such countries as Laos, Cambodia and Vietnam also continue to have serious problems. Taken together, the human rights problems in all these countries, as well as high levels of corruption, often make Singapore and Malaysia look like models for good human rights practices as well as good governance. Nonetheless, it is from the latter two countries that political leaders and their supporters have been most vociferous in their defence of local cultural values, as opposed to 'Western' notions of individual rights. It is in response to these discourses, and to actual human rights problems, that critical actors from within the region as well as from elsewhere – including academics, journalists, policy-makers and human rights activists – have taken issue with some of the basic ideas about the relationship between culture on the one hand, and political issues to do with authority, legitimacy and sovereignty on the other. And these have been at the heart of many of the normative debates in the post-Cold-War period.

Culture and normative theory

Normative theory in IR refers simply to the moral or ethical dimension of activities in the international sphere. But there is nothing simple about the way in which normative arguments and analyses are deployed.

Moreover, the range of practical issues that come within the purview of normative theory is enormous, from intervention to distributive justice, from international legal matters to trade regimes, from nuclear issues to environmental matters, and all manner of human rights and human wrongs from female circumcision to capital punishment. As discussed, however, normative theory has usually been given little attention by realists, especially when combined with the kind of positivist approach that eschews the appropriateness of normative considerations to proper 'scientific' studies. In addition, since for a traditional realist morality can only be enforced within a sovereign sphere, and not under conditions of anarchy where there is no ultimate authority capable of enforcing right behaviour, it cannot be considered as having practical relevance in the international sphere. Since the 1980s, however, there has been a noticeable revival of normative theory to challenge these views. It has been given a particular boost by the growing interest in the role of culture in world politics, a concept that lends itself much more readily to normative than empirical analysis.

The key debates in international normative theory in the post-Cold-War period have revolved largely around two distinct approaches to the human condition – cosmopolitanism and communitarianism. Recall here the discussion in chapter 2, which draws attention to Aristotle's normative commitment to the specific, local political community – the *polis*. This corresponds more or less with a contemporary communitarian position which, as the name suggests, focuses on the moral status and value of particular political communities or states. This contrasts with the notion, first advanced in Stoic philosophy, that there exists a community of humankind – a *cosmopolis* – that transcends local particularities and cultural norms, and has a moral status of its own. Subscribing to a cosmopolitan morality therefore involves a strong sense of moral obligation to people other than our fellow nationals or citizens – in fact to all others, regardless of their membership of particular communities. Given the cosmopolitan commitment to the principle of human equality, this also means that certain obligations extend to every human person, regardless of religion, gender, age, class, cultural affinity or any other particularity. This is the essence of universalism (a term often used synonymously with cosmopolitanism) that is embodied in the notion of universal human rights. In other words, it is simply by virtue of a person's humanity that she or he is regarded as possessing a 'human' right – not because they are a particular *kind* of person.

A culturalist view, however, would have it that people are first and foremost creatures of a particular community, a defining element of which is its culture and which in fact makes its members into *particular kinds* of people. The concept of 'culture' here stands as a marker of particularity – it is what differentiates one community from another. More-over, since norms and values – which include notions of rights and duties – are derived primarily from 'culture' and are not inherent in a universal human psyche, it follows that different cultural communities will have different notions of rights and wrongs, good and evil and so on. Culturalist critics of cosmopolitan morality argue further that the putative subject of universal human rights, the individual person who stands stripped of every shred of their cultural or social context, is a fiction – and one that only Westerners imbued with an Enlightenment mentality are likely to believe in. Non-Western cultures, they argue, simply do not have intellectual traditions that view a person apart from his or her community and cannot therefore readily assimilate the notion of individualism that is essential to the theory of universal human rights. This relativist story is endorsed not only by various kinds of culturalist theorists such as Huntington, but also by various authoritarian elites in non-Western countries who find such accounts of the relationship between culture and morality congenial to their own political projects.

CONCLUSION

For many scholars the Cold War was the most familiar and apparently enduring feature of international political life. It was the foundation from which much theorizing started. Very few assumed that the foundation itself needed questioning. Among the lessons in this, once again, is that one should be alert to the fact that seemingly perennial phenomena can disappear almost overnight. The failure to predict the events of 1989–91 contributed to the more general stirrings of change that had been taking place within the discipline of IR since the early 1980s. While realist theory and positivist methodology remain highly influential in contemporary IR, the post-Cold-War world has been especially conducive to new developments in thinking. As shown above, there has been no shortage of grand ideas about the shape of things to come. From the 'end of history' to the 'clash of civilizations' and the more general role of culture in world politics, there has been a significant flourishing of intellectual ideas since 1989. Among these, normative theory has come to the fore especially, although not exclusively, in relation to 'culture'. In addition, there have been some disturbing trends, especially those revolving around the deadly politics of identity. These, among other things, are implicated in some key issues concerning security and insecurity in the contemporary world, to which I turn next.

5

Security and Insecurity in the Contemporary World

The traditional concept of security in IR has revolved almost exclusively around the state and its survival as a political community. Indeed, the ultimate goal of state behaviour, and its core 'value', is assumed to be the securing of the state itself against anything that may threaten its existence or integrity. Thus the condition of being 'secure', at least in conventional IR terms, is one in which threats to the state are minimal. Security has therefore usually been linked to the military defence of the state and its sovereignty against external threats. For this reason a significant part of security studies has been concerned with 'strategic' studies, or the study of war. The overriding security concerns of the second half of the twentieth century were understandably preoccupied with the possibility of a 'hot' nuclear confrontation between the superpowers and their allies which had the potential not only to kill millions of people in the short term, but to make the planet virtually uninhabitable in the longer term. Strategic aspects of security studies were therefore given a much stronger profile during this period.

State or national security issues, however, have very often involved internal threats as well. Many states in the Cold War period, especially (although not exclusively) those in the former colonial world, were concerned with subversion from within, whether this came in the form of ideological opposition to the government or from ethnic separatist groups. At another level, states like the US also maintained an active security interest in domestic political developments in other countries. Sometimes this went beyond mere interest. Direct, but covert, interference by the Central Intelligence Agency (CIA) in Chile, for example, resulted in the socialist leadership being overthrown in a coup led by General Augusto Pinochet on 11 September 1973. With respect to most 'domestic' matters, however, mainstream security studies in IR, while perhaps acknowledging some of these matters as impacting on the broader field of security concerns, maintained an almost exclusive focus on the external determinants. This was also related to the perceived need to maintain a clear distinction between the 'inside' and the 'outside', the 'domestic' and the 'international', and therefore between what constitutes the legitimate field of IR on the one hand and political science on the other.

Much has changed in the study of security in the post-Cold-War period. The extent to which alternative ways of seeing and understanding the world had emerged before the end of the 1980s, as noted above, applies no less to perceptions of security – and insecurity – than any other aspect of world politics. Liberalism, which has traditionally included peace research approaches, has long provided an important critique of the traditional realist security paradigm. A further useful critique has been developed within the constructivist branch of IR scholarship, while more dissident views are provided by critical theory, feminist and postmodern approaches. But first I revisit aspects of realism in order to set out the fundamentals of the dominant approaches to security in the Cold War period, so that the reader can then better appreciate the ways in which alternative approaches not only seek to understand the world, but to transform it. I then go on to consider how current concerns, such as humanitarian issues on the one hand and terrorism on the other, can best be analysed in terms of the contemporary framework for security studies.

Realist perspectives on security

Certain realist approaches to IR developed a set of beliefs about the nature of the world that rest on certain basic assumptions about the human condition. These include a rather pessimistic view of human nature, one that sees humans as at once fearful and self-regarding. In turn, this feeds into a theory of power politics and the struggle for survival in a dangerous and irredeemably anarchic world. Graham Evans and Jeffrey Newnham (1998, p. 565) write that war, defined as 'direct, somatic violence between state actors' is considered by realists as intrinsic to the international system, and that this idea is the 'distinctive hallmark of realism'. The *political* element of warfare as an instrument of state policy has been most famously summarized by the Prussian theorist of war Karl von Clausewitz (1780–1831), who argued that: 'War is not merely a political act, but also a real political instrument, a continuation of political commerce, a carrying out of the same by other means.' But Clausewitz also drew attention to the 'primordial' aspects of the enterprise, arguing that the 'original violence of its elements' include 'hatred and animosity, which may be looked upon as blind instinct' (Clausewitz [1832], 1968, pp. 119–20).

The concept of state security is tied to the general scenario described above, especially with respect to the condition of anarchy and its negative consequences. The sovereign state becomes the ultimate guarantor of people's security. Wrapped in the protective mantle of sovereignty, people can find a measure of security that is simply unattainable under other conditions. Thus the state is the primary source of protection for individuals and sub-state groups. This leads directly to the notion that it is the *duty* of the state to provide this protection, not only from external threats but from within as well. And should the sovereign power and its agents themselves become the major source of threat to people's security, then people are entitled to withdraw their support from the sovereign and defend themselves. As mentioned in chapter 2, even under the relative authoritarian conditions of the Hobbesian state, people retain in principle the fundamental right of self-preservation, since it is for the purpose of self-preservation that they have submitted to the sovereign authority in the first place. Interestingly, there are important aspects of this argument that are perfectly compatible with contemporary notions of human security.

For structural realists or neorealists, however, primordialist theories which seek to explain the propensity for aggression and violence in terms of human nature are relegated in favour of an account that places far more emphasis on the *structural* aspects of international anarchy. Human nature still has a role to play, but it is the capacity for calculated action that is emphasized rather than some kind of primordial urge. Even so, there is plenty of room for miscalculation. Related to this is the idea of the 'security dilemma' which, as discussed above, was prominent during the Cold War period. This involves a perception of the intentions of states on the one hand, and an assessment of their material military capabilities on the other. The dilemma arises when the action of one state in enhancing its military capacity, and hence its overall security, causes another state (or states) to feel threatened or less secure. The first state may intend only to enhance its defensive, not offensive, capabilities. But it will not necessarily be seen in this way by other states who may then set about further enhancing their own military capacities to meet what they perceive as a threat. The first state may react, in turn, by further enhancing its capabilities, again prompting further action by other states, and so a spiralling pattern of military build-up is created.

There are, however, ways and means of containing the dilemma. A liberal institutionalist approach, for example, would point to the possibilities available through co-operative security measures. But from a mainstream neorealist viewpoint, although amelioration is possible, there can be no permanent solution. Once again, this is dictated by the structural imperatives of the international system of states. Moreover, where peaceful relations do prevail in the realist world of international politics, this is more often than not seen in negative terms simply as the absence of violent conflict rather than a positive condition in itself. An ultra-realist position would in fact view warfare as more or less 'natural', while peace – where and when it exists, and however desirable it may be – is more of an artificially induced condition. More specifically, a world at peace would be one in which a certain equilibrium or a 'balance of power' had been achieved – and this could only ever be viewed as a temporary, if fortuitous, phenomenon.

With the collapse of the former Soviet Empire the structural conditions of bipolarity which supported a form of balance of power also gave way. What has replaced it has been a matter of debate, but some would argue that rather than a multipolar system forming, there is a situation of hegemony in which the US, supported by powerful allies, holds a position of unrivalled dominance. Arguably, this has bred, in some quarters, a spirit of resentment and hostility towards the West in general and the US in particular. It is worth noting here that anti-Westernism has been manifest for some time throughout much of the former colonial world but was somewhat muted during the Cold War period. The 'Asian values' debate, discussed in chapter 4, although led principally by countries allied with the US against communism during the Cold War, was one clear manifestation of this resentment. More aggressive and violent displays have been evident in so-called 'Islamic fundamentalist' movements and organizations (I say 'so-called' because the religion of Islam is often used more as a vehicle for politics for many organizations, rather than representing a cause in itself).

It is important to emphasize once again that not all those who regard themselves as 'realists' share identical views on the outlook for security and insecurity, or on other aspects of IR. Some have a much more optimistic outlook on the possibilities for security co-operation among states, believing that the present period is one in which a condition of 'mature anarchy' may emerge (Buzan, 2/1991, p. 176). In this, states act on the realization that their security objectives may be best achieved by abandoning a narrow self-interested approach and taking account of the security interests of other states. A co-operative situation may develop in which groups of countries form a 'security community'. The EU is an obvious example. The idea of transcending narrow self-interest and engaging in co-operative security projects, however, is more usually associated with liberal approaches.

The liberal security order

From a liberal viewpoint, the end of the Cold War presented a wealth of new opportunities for international co-operation, requiring only the exercise of political will among key players to bring about an unprecedented level of international peace and security. The basis for this scenario is provided by international institutions designed to ameliorate the conditions of anarchy, largely through the practice of collective security. This general approach, known as 'liberal institutionalism', therefore accepts aspects of realism – at least in so far as it accepts anarchy as a feature of the international system – but believes that this condition can be ultimately controlled via the establishment of a durable network of international institutions underpinned by strongly supported norms and rules. As with the idea of mature anarchy, then, this liberal viewpoint subscribes to the possibility of a managed anarchy.

The League of Nations represented an early attempt to institutionalize the principles of collective security at an international level. Along with the peaceful settlement of disputes, it was also meant to foster trade and other objectives supportive of international security. That the League ultimately failed in its prime objectives is of course history. However, its failure did not mean that the basic objectives were unattainable. The circumstances of the time, and the lack of political will among the major players to shake off old habits of statecraft and *make* the system work, all conspired against the chances of success for this particular regime. Its successor, the UN, has enjoyed a much greater degree of success. The UN's central organ, the Security Council, has enabled it to act more decisively than its predecessor. This is because although the five permanent members of the Security Council (Great Britain, France, Russia, China and the US) have the right of veto on any particular decision, they also have the right to abstain. In other words, an inflexible principle of unanimity has not been built into the decision-making mechanism. Even so, it has been argued that the UN was severely constrained in its pursuit of collective security by the conditions of the Cold War. In contrast, during the early post-Cold-War period there was a significant growth in confidence concerning its capabilities, especially in the wake of the Gulf War. For example, George Bush, then US President, famously declared before a joint session of the US Congress in September 1990:

> Out of these troubled times . . . a new world order can emerge; a new
> era freer from the threat of terror, stronger in the pursuit of justice,

and more secure in the quest for peace, an era in which the nations of the world, East and West, North and South, can prosper and live in harmony. . . . We are now in sight of a United Nations that performs as envisioned by its founders. (quoted in Roberts, 1991, p. 519)

Subsequent UN-sponsored activities, however, have met with varying degrees of success (or failure). Apart from the Gulf War, most of its security-related activities have been specifically in the area of peace-keeping in 'internal' conflict situations – that is, with conflicts occurring within the borders of states rather than between states. This has some-times been seen as beyond the competence of the UN, given that its primary role is with respect to inter-, not intra-, state conflict. In other words, the mandate of the UN is concerned with international, not national, security issues. However, this view has been criticized for being too narrow in its understanding of what constitutes a threat to interna-tional peace and security, and far too rigid in drawing a distinct bound-ary between the national and the international spheres. After all, most internal conflicts have significant spill-over effects, not least in their tendency to generate large-scale flows of refugees which then become the responsibility of the international community at large. Similar points have been made with respect to environmental issues, many of which may originate in a particular state but which often have significant regional or global consequences.

Other aspects of the UN's role in contributing to world order, espe-cially in terms of global governance, are considered in the next chapter. For the moment I must note that the UN is the pre-eminent international organization with a responsibility for global security. Other institutions directly involved in international security include NATO. As already noted, NATO was founded in 1949 in the wake of the Berlin crisis and is obviously a Cold War institution. But it has found a new *raison d'être* in the post-Cold-War security order, especially in relation to Eastern Europe. NATO's military action against Serbia in defence of ethnic Albanian Kosovars has been analysed in terms of 'humanitarian inter-vention' – another concept that has gained increasing prominence in the contemporary period and which represents a significant departure from conventional norms of conduct in that it explicitly circumvents or under-mines state sovereignty. I return to this issue shortly.

There is insufficient space to do more than mention just a few other organizations that have either an explicit or implicit international secu-rity function. Many of these, like NATO, are regional rather than global. Others include the African Union and the Association of South-East Asian Nations (ASEAN). In addition there are numerous ongoing exper-iments in regional integration in most parts of the world. The most advanced is the EU, which is still in the process of expanding and deepening. Closely related to this is the Organization for Security and Co-operation in Europe (OSCE). A spin-off from ASEAN is the ASEAN Regional Forum (ARF), which also has a specific security function. Some of these institutions were originally designed, at least in part, to 'balance' the perceived power – either military or economic or both – of other large blocs or countries.

Whether designed specifically with economic integration or security issues in mind, the growth of these and other such organizations are seen as constituting an international institutional network, the net effect of which is to enhance the prospects for building a durable regime of international peace and security in the twenty-first century. Far from being a utopian dream, liberal institutionalists believe that this is an eminently attainable objective. The circumstances under which it may be realized, however, depend not merely on the political will of key actors in building and maintaining such institutions, and remaining committed to the ideals that underpin them. According to some observers, it may also depend on the institutionalization of another kind of liberal political ideal throughout the world – and that is the institution of democratic government.

Some of the discussion in chapters 3 and 4 has already referred to the democratic peace thesis put forward by various thinkers from Kant onwards. The thesis is addressed primarily to relations between states, and this accords with traditional approaches to security. But there are aspects of 'domestic' democratic theory and practice that are highly relevant to security issues as well. These are concerned mainly with what goes on within the borders of states. However, as with many so-called domestic issues, there are significant implications for the international or global sphere as well. The main point to be noted here is that democratic constitutional political institutions are, virtually by definition, committed to the peaceful resolution of conflict. People in democratic states do not engage in violent conflict in order to endorse or change their governments – they vote. Democratic governments do not generally imprison, torture or murder their political opponents. They must not only tolerate them, but allow them to *become* the government if that is the verdict of the polls. And both sides – or all sides – must agree to play by the constitutional rules. Democracy is, in effect, the institutionalization of peaceful conflict.

Perhaps one of the most salient aspects from a security viewpoint is that democratic governments do not murder their own citizens in large numbers (see Rummel, 1997) – the practice of capital punishment in a number of democratic states notwithstanding. Some may argue that all this has little to do with IR, but given the kinds of humanitarian issue that have claimed a prominent place on the global security agenda in the last few years precisely because of the behaviour of murderous regimes, this position is increasingly difficult to sustain. Genocide and ethnic cleansing, as happened in Rwanda and the former Yugoslavia during the 1990s, were issues that the 'international community' could scarcely ignore, or pretend were matters for these states to resolve themselves behind the veil of sovereignty.

To summarize some of the points of comparison between realist and liberal viewpoints on international security, although they clearly diverge in a number of respects, it is often more a question of degree, or an ordering of principles that marks one off from the other. For example, liberals do not deny the anarchic character of the international sphere, nor do most realists dispute that institutions have value. Both subscribe to the notion of the security dilemma, and all but the narrowest of realists would say that democratic norms have no relevance at all. More generally, although the pessimism of realism versus the optimism of liberalism about the prospects for international peace and security can be represented as polar opposites, in practice most on either 'side' would say that the difference is one of emphasis, albeit often a strong one, rather than a complete antithesis. Moreover, both realists and liberals have traditionally stood firm on one important common ground, and that is the centrality of the state to the international system and as the prime object of security. There are other approaches to security and insecurity in the contemporary world, however, which generally seek to transcend the state-centricity of both. And in doing so they also have some interesting things to say about methodology.

Alternative approaches to security and insecurity

Recognizing the 'reality' of the world is, according to a traditionalist realist view, a matter of recognizing brute facts for what they are, and not being misled by wishful thinking about unattainable goals. This claims to represent an objective reality as opposed to the subjective, value-laden approach of liberals. Moreover, its apparent common-sense outlook has been widely regarded as essential to the proper understanding of security issues. On the other hand, the strong normative elements embodied in liberalism have sometimes been seen as contributing to *in*security if moral principle is put ahead of self-regarding, prudential considerations. But the realist and liberal positions on security and other issues do not exhaust the alternatives.

Constructivism rejects the notion that there is a body of objective knowledge about the world that exists independently of subjective understandings. While agreeing that there are certain empirical facts about the world, the interpretation of these facts – the way in which they are invested with meaning – is scarcely an objective exercise. The 'reality' of the world, which includes the world of international relations, has been socially constructed via a complex of inter-subjective understandings. This means that the condition of anarchy is, quite simply, 'what states make of it' (Wendt, 1992, p. 395). In other words, anarchy, as the prime structural feature of the international sphere around which all considerations of security and insecurity revolve, is not an autonomous phenomenon that generates its own inescapable logic. This also means that the security dilemma, for example, does not exist *before* any interaction between states but is in fact a *product* of the social interactions of states. According to Wendt, one of the main purposes in mounting this argument is to support the liberal claim that institutions can indeed be devised so as to transform state interests and identities and therefore create conditions more conducive to international peace and security (ibid., p. 394).

Constructivist security theory has also addressed the idea of 'security communities' in some detail, the original idea for which was first developed by Karl Deutsch in the 1950s in relation to the North Atlantic region and which emphasized the efficacy of shared understandings, norms and values that could develop among states (see Deutsch, 1957). There are some similarities with democratic peace theory here, but constructivist approaches do not limit their idea of community to democracies. A basic premise of contemporary constructivist theory is that global politics has an essentially *social* character, in contrast with the firmly *a*social world depicted by neorealist scholars. This brings into prominence 'the need to consider the importance of state identities and the sources of state interests; suggesting that the purposes for which power is deployed and is regarded as socially legitimate may be changing; and positing that the cultural similarities among states may be shaped by institutional agents' (Adler and Barnett, 1998, p. 12).

Another more radical challenge to conventional thinking on security that shifts the focus away from states, while also deploying ideas about the social construction of reality, has been provided by feminist theories. I mentioned earlier that feminist critics of traditional IR approaches regarded these as irredeemably masculinist in their basic assumptions. This is especially so with respect to security, which has traditionally been viewed in highly masculinist military terms. J. Ann Tickner argues that international politics with its focus on state security has always been a highly gendered activity: 'Since foreign and military policy-making has been largely conducted by men, the discipline that analyzes these activities is bound to be primarily about men and masculinity.' She also points out that women and men are socialized into believing that 'war and power politics are spheres of activity with which men have a special affinity and that their voices in describing and prescribing for this world are likely to be more authentic (Tickner, 1992, p. 4). And, as in many other fields of thought, 'we have become accustomed to equating what is human with what is male' (ibid.). Put another way, what we regard as 'normal' human behaviour is usually based on a male model of normality. But maleness or masculinity is not as straightforward as one might think at first glance. Tickner, among other feminist theorists, agrees that the model of masculinity adopted in traditional security approaches is based on an ideal model of a male warrior possessed of ruggedness, courage, strength and bravado, and not that many 'real' men actually fit this stereotype either (ibid., p. 6, citing Connell, 1995).

What might a feminist security agenda look like then? And what kinds of insights might a gender-sensitive viewpoint bring to bear on security and insecurity in the contemporary world? First and foremost, feminist analysis draws attention to the pervasiveness of gender hierarchies and the extent to which these impinge on the lives of women, including their vital interests in forms of security that may well be written off by men as not 'real' security issues. A recent example, which has attracted a great deal of publicity and which is now much more widely recognized as a genuine security concern, is the widespread practice of rape of women in war. This recognition would have been much more difficult, however, if feminism had not at the same time succeeded in breaking down some of the barriers between the rigid separation of 'domestic' or 'private' concerns and 'public' ones. Rape, like incest, was for a long time one of those things that many people simply would not talk about; relegating it to a non-public realm was a very effective avoidance strategy.

Another manifestation of the gender hierarchy with implications for women's security is the profound inequality that exists around the world in terms of economic status and power. A recent compendium of statistics reveals the extent to which poverty, violence, ill-health, poor working conditions, lack of legal protection and general cultural attitudes afflict women's lives around the globe. These statistics range from the finding that two out of every three of the world's illiterate people are women, to a report that between 250,000 and 400,000 women were raped during the 1972 war for independence in Bangladesh, to a study which estimates that women own about 1 per cent of the world's land (Seager, 2/1997). Although the statistics for women in the Third World are worse on most counts, those for the advanced industrialized nations show that women there continue to lag well behind men. This indicates an ongoing problem of subordination embedded in a particular masculinist 'construction of reality' with multiple social and economic consequences. Although some of these issues seem to have little to do with 'international security' as such, feminists argue that they simply cannot be bracketed off as irrelevant. The distribution, or rather *mal*distribution, of resources – which can occur on the basis not only of gender, but also of class, religion, language, ethnicity and age – is regarded as a serious security issue by various international agencies, especially those concerned with development. Of course feminists are not the only people to have drawn attention to these more general matters, but it is indicative of the kind of broad security agenda with which feminists are concerned.

Critical theory, like feminism, rejects the emphasis placed on the state and takes in a much broader array of factors. As critical theory is closely related to Marxist or socialist political viewpoints, a key focus for critique is global capitalism. In that it generates relentless competition for materials and resources, it is global capitalism and not anarchy that must be held primarily responsible for much conflict and violence, whether this takes place within or between states. Certain strands of critical theory are, however, very much concerned with the behaviour of states – not so much in their relations with each other, but in terms of how they treat their own inhabitants. Given that it is now widely acknowledged that people are much more likely to suffer at the hands of their own governments than from any external threat, critical theorists argue that attention needs to be shifted from the security of the state as such, to the security of the groups and individuals within it. Unlike older school Marxists, contemporary critical theorists recognize that people within a state do not simply constitute socio-economic 'classes'. Gender, religion, language, ethnicity and age are recognized as highly relevant – and this is comparable with the range of factors on which feminists focus.

For critical theorists, any security agenda worth its name must be primarily concerned with the quest for human emancipation. This entails adopting a methodology that is addressed not merely to problem-solving within the parameters of the existing social, economic and political order, with the aim of simply ameliorating the worst excesses, but to a more thorough *transformation* of that order to achieve the greatest possible measure of security through human equality. Critical theory, like feminism, therefore has a very strong normative thrust. And it is by no means content simply to understand the world, but very much concerned with changing it. Another point to note is that the focus on emancipation renders critical theory a progressive, modernist political project with roots in Enlightenment philosophy.

Postmodernism encompasses a number of different approaches. In IR and security studies, however, a common set of propositions is discernible. Once again, a prime target of critique is realism (and neorealism), although most other approaches are rejected as well for their modernist underpinnings. The realist view of the world is regarded as a 'meta-narrative'. The task of the postmodernist is to 'deconstruct' this meta-narrative, thereby revealing its own subjective foundations. As noted above, a meta-narrative is meant, at least by those who construct it, to represent a universal Truth. Postmodernists will have none of this. There are no eternal truths, and even trivial 'facts' are suspect. The world is socially constructed and its 'reality' is open to as many different interpretations as there are people to make them. There is no truth or reality beyond these acts of interpretation, no body of knowledge – social scientific or otherwise – that has a shred of objectivity, and no possibility of devising universal solutions to problems of human emancipation. Where certain 'knowledges' do prevail, this is simply a function of power. For example, it is the power of the US in contemporary international politics that is imposing a 'truth' or 'meta-narrative' about terrorism – and the appropriate responses to it. Alternative interpretations of what constitutes terrorism may hold that it is actually the US, rather than other groups, that is guilty of terrorist crimes. Once again, it is only the power of the US that ensures that its interpretation prevails over other possible interpretations. There is certainly no 'objective truth' about guilt or innocence in this respect, only deeply subjective interpretative positions.

Given its particular concern to deconstruct the realist meta-narrative, a particular focus of postmodern IR analysis revolves around the state, sovereignty and state-centrism. In terms of security, as described above, for realists of virtually any stripe, security questions revolve almost exclusively around the state. Postmodern discussions of security, like most of the other approaches, therefore seek to decentre the state as well as notions such as citizenship (which are tied to the state paradigm), and propose to broaden the scope of enquiry to include other possible forms of community and identity that might require 'security'. Very often, it is *against* the state that struggles for security are being carried out around the contemporary world. This brings me to the idea of human security and although at least some postmodernists might reject the essential 'humanism' of this particular security project, it nonetheless speaks to many of the concerns raised by postmodernists as well as by most of the other alternative approaches to security.

The human security paradigm

The idea of human security encompasses a range of concerns that take the concept of security into almost every area of human life. The origin of the idea can be traced to the 1960s (Tow and Trood, 2000, p. 17), and was reflected in the new security literature that began to emerge in the 1980s and 1990s (see, for example, Booth, 1991). It has been given much of its recent currency by the United Nations *Human Development Report 1994*, which provided a major statement on the new security concept. The report argued that traditional definitions had been far too narrow, with the concept being largely confined to 'security of territory from external aggression, or as the protection of national interests in foreign policy or as global security from the threat of nuclear holocaust'. Forgotten in all this were the more basic concerns 'of ordinary people who sought security in their daily lives' (UNDP, 1994, p. 22). Human security was defined generally in terms of safety from chronic threats such as hunger, disease and repression as well as 'protection from sudden and hurtful disruptions in the patterns of daily life – whether in homes, in jobs or in communities' (ibid., p. 23).

A more specific list of seven security concerns was also provided: economic security – consisting, for example, of freedom from poverty; food security – access to basic sustenance; health security – access to health care and protection from disease; environmental security – protection against pollution and depletion; personal security – including safety from war, torture, sexual and other forms of assault including domestic violence; community security – referring to the integrity and survival of traditional cultures and minorities; and political security – the protection of civil and political rights. A question that has often been raised in response to this very comprehensive list is: what human ailment or problem is *not* considered to be a security issue? Even granted that each one is a legitimate security concern of one kind or another, a further question many would pose is whether they can all be considered as issues that are properly the concern of *international* security studies. Here, the answer depends very much on what school of thought one subscribes to. Realists would obviously embrace very few, while most critical and postmodern responses would admit most, if not all, to the realm of legitimate international security concerns. This reflects, among other things, the critical and postmodern rejection of the rigid dividing line between the domestic and the international as well as between the various disciplines – IR, political science, sociology and so forth.

It is clear, then, that the concept of human security has a great many implications, from how one thinks about the legitimate domain of IR to what can be considered a genuine security issue for either national or international attention, or both. One of the more specific fields for which it has particular importance is human rights. Here the shift from 'state security' to 'human security' has encouraged a more sustained focus on the fact that human rights abuses – which range from torture, arbitrary arrest and detention to sheer neglect of basic sustenance needs – not only constitute a serious security issue, but often occur as a direct or indirect result of state-sponsored activities. Political repression has often been justified by reference to 'national security' – and still is by most authoritarian countries. Singapore's 'total security doctrine', for example, links internal political subversion directly to national security. Internal political oppression has also been justified at times by the US, one of the most famous episodes being the communist witch-hunt led by Senator Joseph McCarthy in the 1950s. The more recent 'war on terror' is another development that concerns not only the actions of the US abroad, but the worry among civil liberties groups that it will be used to justify new methods of oppression at home.

In summary, human rights abuses have often been defended on the grounds that they are justified by the ends they served – and that is the greater good served by securing the 'national interest'. This is sometimes referred to in moral theory as a 'consequentialist' argument. In other words, one looks to the ultimate consequences of an action in order to judge whether it is right or wrong – in which case the means may justify the end. However, this approach goes directly against another key moral position, articulated most clearly by Kant and adhered to today by moral theorists known as 'deontologists', and that is the principle that people must never be treated as a means to an end. Each and every human is an end in him or herself. This is a species of rule-based moral theory that also underlies principles of international law (see Mapel and Nardin, 1992, p. 297). Today, it is less common to hear arguments that the national interest should be invoked to justify cruel, degrading or repressive treatment of groups or individuals by the state or its agents. This move is clearly consistent with the recognition that human rights are not equivalent to states' rights and, indeed, that the pursuit of so-called states' rights or a narrowly defined national interest has often been at the expense of the very people that states are supposed to protect, namely their own citizens. For if the modern theory of sovereignty imposes any moral duties on states, it is surely the security and well-being of their own people. Moreover, this accords with the Hobbesian focus on the security of people within the state and the duty of protection owed by the sovereign.

I have so far discussed a number of the theoretical issues to do with security as well as some of their practical implications. There are many others that could be raised, but given that this is a *short* introduction to the subject of IR, it must suffice to mention just two more. The first is the issue of humanitarian intervention in 'internal' conflicts. The second concerns terrorism and the nature of responses to it, especially with respect to the events of 11 September 2001 and their aftermath.

Humanitarian intervention

The term 'intervention' in IR denotes some kind of intrusion into the internal affairs of a state by an external actor – usually another state, group of states, international organization or even a sub-state or non-state group. On occasions, intervention may be officially permitted or condoned by authorities within the subject state. This is usually the case with international peace-keeping activities. The intervention in East Timor by Australian, New Zealand and other forces in 2000, which was permitted (albeit somewhat reluctantly) by Indonesia, is one example. But at other times it will be specifically aimed against a governing authority as, for example, in the case of NATO intervention in Kosovo against the Serbs and, more recently, the US-led 'coalition against terrorism' that drove the Taliban from government in Afghanistan. These are obviously cases of *forcible* intervention and therefore need to be distinguished from voluntary acceptance of intervention illustrated by the East Timor case. Forcible intervention, whether on humanitarian grounds or otherwise is obviously directly contrary to the doctrine of non-intervention in the domestic affairs of states which emerged as a norm of international politics with the Peace of Westphalia along with the principle of sovereignty, and is enshrined in the UN Charter. Given the history of inter-state warfare, it is not difficult to see why so much importance has been placed on this doctrine.

The twin principles of sovereignty and non-intervention, however, have been weakened considerably in the contemporary period. Again, the end of the Cold War and the changing international environment has contributed much to this change. As the prospect of major inter-state warfare appeared to fade into history, much more attention was given to the deadly internal conflicts being fought around the globe. The UN Secretary-General of the early post-Cold-War period, Boutros Boutros-Ghali, in a major report to the Security Council entitled *Agenda for Peace*, said that although the prospects for common international progress with respect to peace and security remained firmly grounded in respect for the fundamental sovereignty and integrity of states, the sovereignty principle needed to be reassessed and balanced by a legitimate ethical concern for what goes on inside the borders of states. This meant including on the international security agenda issues of human rights and good governance along with the empowerment of the poor and the marginalized (cited in Lawson, 1995, pp. 4–5).

The 'humanitarian' label that has been attached to various instances of intervention in the contemporary period provides the essential normative justification that proponents would argue trumps the doctrine of inviolable state sovereignty. This was clearly the argument used by the

NATO-led coalition against Serbia, with the focus of humanitarian concern being Albanian Kosovars. The peace-keeping operation that followed, however, has been as much concerned with providing security for Serb Kosovars against revenge attacks. This shows the fluidity of the identity of victims and perpetrators in crisis situations. Also subject to fluid interpretations are the circumstances under which an act of intervention is humanitarian or not. This cannot depend simply on the say-so of those doing the intervening. For example, it is widely believed that French intervention in Rwanda in 1994 was motivated almost exclusively by self-(national) interest to do with France's perception of its interests and status in Africa, even though the sole justification put forward was humanitarian principle.

Although from a human rights viewpoint there are good reasons for supporting the norm of humanitarian intervention in certain situations against the norm of inviolable sovereignty, the question remains as to who is entitled to adjudicate in any particular case. One answer may be the United Nations, which can claim to enjoy a high level of legitimacy in this respect. But there are aspects of this question that go beyond standard measures of legitimacy and authority. Chris Brown points out that intervention is always an act of power. In the present period, the rich and powerful states – namely the US and its allies – get to determine just when intervention is appropriate or not, as well as what counts as 'humanitarian'. He concludes that 'one does not have to be an apologist for tyranny to see that this is not a particularly desirable state of affairs' (Brown, 2002, p. 153). Another commentator notes that, in the case of Kosovo, what NATO claimed to be an act of 'humanitarian intervention' was regarded by critics as 'coercive diplomacy' at best and an example of 'state-sponsored international terrorism' at worst (Stern, 2000, p. 96). This brings me to the final topic of this chapter.

Terrorism

Among the most recent cases of intervention that have dominated discussions of security and insecurity were, first, the terrorist attacks of 11 September 2001 on US targets and, second, the response by the US, supported by a significant international coalition, in forcibly intervening to unseat the Taliban government in Afghanistan in the belief that it had been harbouring the organization responsible for the attacks. There is no question that, however one defines international terrorism, the attacks on the World Trade Center in New York and the Pentagon in Washington DC that day in 2001 constitute a prime case. Nonetheless, it is important to note that this type of attack is not a typical case. Many terrorist attacks are aimed at domestic regimes or other targets within the terrorists' own country. Various separatist groups, whether from the Basque country or Kashmir, and similar movements within Northern Ireland, Peru, Sri Lanka, the Philippines and Israel, to name a few, have used terror tactics to further their political objectives. A number of terrorist organizations, or occasionally individuals acting alone, link political objectives to a religious cause, and none of the major religions has been exempt. Hinduism, Christianity, Judaism and Islam have all, at one time or another, inspired causes in which terrorism has been justified as a means to a righteous end.

In the recent past much of the focus has been on the use of terrorism by various groups to advance Islamist objectives, namely, the total Islamization of politics and society. Many of these groups harbour strong anti-Western or anti-US sentiments as well. The history and sociology of these movements is complex and a thorough understanding of them would require keen attention to the colonial past, neo-colonialism, US, British and French foreign policy and so on. Indeed, attention to these factors is far more important than attention to 'religion' as such. Osama bin Laden may have invoked the name of Allah in every other sentence uttered in his video features, and his followers are certainly inspired by a fervent religiosity, but the objectives of his al-Qaida network are essentially political. Moreover, as most Muslims would point out, there is nothing in Islam that justifies the use of terror tactics of any kind.

The recent focus on the Islamic sources of terrorism has tended to overshadow other forms of terrorism, including those linked to the obsessions of particular individuals who may act alone or lead small but deadly groups of devotees. These are as likely to be found within America as anywhere else. In 1995 Tim McVeigh, the 'Oklahoma bomber', and before him the infamous 'Unabomber' Theodore Kaczynski are typical of the loner types and are sometimes regarded as representative of an almost uniquely American type of paranoid terrorist. There is also the Ku Klux Klan – not generally regarded as a terrorist organization, although the people that it targets have every reason to view it as such. It also fits a general definition of terrorism in a number of respects: 'The use or threatened use of violence on a systematic basis to achieve political objectives'. Characteristic traits of terrorism are 'fear-inducement, ruthlessness, a disregard for established humanitarian values and an unquenchable thirst for publicity', while strategy or methods 'commonly include hijacking, hostage-taking, bombings, indiscriminate shootings, assassinations and mass murders' (Evans and Newnham, 1998, p. 530). This definition, then, could be applied to a variety of groups and individuals with a variety of causes, grudges and ambitions. And whatever particular tactics are used, there is no question for a terrorist that the end justifies the means.

In looking at the sources of terrorism, although one can point to the grievances of specific groups, there is no simple explanation. An account of the causes of 'Islamic terrorism' would, as mentioned above, involve attention to a complex of factors including colonial legacies, the Palestinian issue, the political economy of the Middle East oil industry, control of water resources, the politics of Islamic groups versus the state (and vice versa) in right-wing, pro-US regimes in the Arab world, the conditions of postcolonialism, and so forth. The anti-state projects of, say, Basque and Irish Republican Army (IRA) groups also have their different histories, although they can be classified together to some extent in that they both belong to minorities that have historically suffered oppression at the hands of a state controlled by another group. On the other hand, there is the phenomenon of state-sponsored terrorism in which a state takes an active, if covert, role in organizing terrorist activities against another state or group within a state – even within their own state. The US has pointed a finger at a number of states over the years, including Libya, Syria and Iran as well as Afghanistan. But the US has frequently been accused of sponsoring terrorism too, both at the level of the state as well as of resistance groups, in protecting its perceived interests in Latin America, Africa, the Middle East and Asia.

Despite the nature of the 11 September attacks, just over a year ago as this book was going to press, one should nonetheless question whether terrorism is likely to become a major source of international insecurity. As already noted, most acts of terrorism are confined to the intra-state sphere, and that is unlikely to change. Writing before the World Trade Center and Pentagon attacks, Fred Halliday argued that terrorism had not become a major international phenomenon in the sense of provoking inter-state conflict or seriously challenging the workings of the international system: 'It is dramatic, cruel, sudden but not . . . a challenge to global order' (Halliday, 2001, p. 51). Things have changed to the extent that the 11 September attack *did* provoke an inter-state conflict. Its implications for global order in the longer term, however, are as yet unclear. But it has certainly focused attention on aspects of national security in daily life, from air travel to the security of major infrastructural facilities. Many people, at least in the US, also live with a heightened sense of fear relating to the possibility of biological or chemical attacks as well as conventional ones. President George W. Bush has implemented an agenda for 'Homeland Security', setting up a special office for the purpose of guarding against non-traditional attacks, including 'cyber' attacks. At the same time, the events of 11 September have given Bush both the political and moral ground on which to move forward with the controversial Missile Defense System (MDS) to provide against the possibility of more conventional attacks.

In the wider scheme of things one must ask what can be done to bring about lasting solutions to the problems of both national and international terrorism. It is one thing to hunt down particular groups of terrorists. It is another to institute defensive programmes of 'Homeland Security'. But it is another thing altogether to address the basic causes of terrorism. For the more reflective observers, these are to be found in adverse conditions of material deprivation and political oppression, combined with a strong sense of injustice against either governing authorities within a state or against an international hegemonic power that is perceived to be at least partly responsible for those adverse conditions of life and the loss of dignity and respect that goes with it. According to this view, any effective 'war against terrorism' must recognize these factors as basic, and implement long-term preventative measures aimed at alleviating the social conditions that breed terrorism in the first place. Others would suggest that, at the same time, states as powerful as the US must look at their own record of covert involvement with terrorism and reject it as a tool of foreign policy in the future.

CONCLUSION

Security and insecurity in the contemporary period clearly have many facets, only a few of which have been touched on in this chapter. What I have sought to do is provide a broad outline of various approaches with a particular emphasis on alternative theoretical approaches to security and insecurity as well as some of the more serious practical issues confronting both scholars and policy-makers today. It should be evident, however, that none of the theories mentioned here is in any way disconnected from political practice in the 'real' world. Indeed, the theorizing of security, as well as the theorizing of IR more generally, in all the various approaches, is intimately connected to actual developments on the ground. Another point emphasized here is that although military security in terms of defending 'the state' is likely to remain a prime referent for security, other non-traditional security issues and approaches are now firmly on the agenda for IR.

6

Global Governance and World Order

The idea – and ideal – of order has been central to theories of politics for centuries, but in the modern period it has revolved almost exclusively around the sovereign state which, as discussed above, first emerged in Europe and later spread around the world via colonization and decolonization. The concept of *international* order therefore takes this sovereign state as its primary unit, which is in turn the basis of a *system* providing for the ordering of relations among the units. The terms 'world order' and 'global order' are often used interchangeably with 'international order'. But whereas the latter denotes a relatively conventional, narrow approach, with states as the basic units of the system, 'world' and 'global' are potentially more inclusive, leaving open the question of which units may be relevant. However, for many theorists, the sovereign state system not only constitutes the essential basis for international order, but actually promotes order in the sense that it provides for structured stability under conditions of anarchy. Therefore order as an ideal – as a value in itself – is connected very closely to order as presently constituted by the sovereign state system.

The concept of order is also implicit in the term 'governance', although the latter need not be connected exclusively to the sovereign state system. In fact, global governance in some ways transcends the state system. And while governance may involve government, it is not synonymous with it, especially in the international sphere. Government, in the usual understanding of the term, is closely associated with formal political rule within a state. 'Governance' is a more expansive concept and, as mentioned in chapter 1, global governance should not be confused with the idea of world government, a different beast altogether. This becomes apparent when one looks at the variety of organizations, regimes and movements which come under the broad umbrella of the global governance concept. These range from the UN and its many agencies to a whole variety of multinational corporations and NGOs. The global governance concept also includes broad structures such as the international human rights regime, which consists of a plethora of organizations both official and unofficial. For this reason, global governance institutions also embrace certain elements of global civil society. In short, global governance is multilayered and pluralistic, embracing a significant range of actors. It was once described as a 'theme in need of a focus' (Groom, 1994, p. 81), although that may be an advantage rather than a shortcoming since flexibility rather than focus ensures greater inclusiveness.

Behind many international organizations concerned with issues of global governance and world order, especially those involved with human rights, the peace movement the environmental movement and the global protest movement, lies a distinct normative theme that puts a premium on the notion of a common humanity with common concerns, needs and interests. The normative aspects of global governance and world order therefore involve an orientation to the common good that transcends state boundaries and the traditional emphasis on the principle of state sovereignty and strict non-intervention. This implies a global ethic not simply of order, but of justice too, as reflected in the cosmopolitan approach to normative international theory. In turn, this raises the question of whether order is a necessary condition for the achievement of justice. Or is order in itself a form of justice? These are some of the questions addressed by international society theorists who have made an important contribution to the normative debate on world order.

The idea of international society

'International society' as a form of world order may be understood as a situation in which states do more than simply coexist in an international system, for the notion of 'society' implies a quality of interaction among its members that reflects a certain measure of shared interests and values. As shown in chapter 3, international society theory was developed largely by English School theorists in the post-war period of the twentieth century. It emphasizes the extent to which effective social order among states is possible under conditions of anarchy. The idea of international society also has very clear normative elements. As Tim Dunne

(1998, p. 10) notes, international society theorists do not assume that states are 'strangers to the moral world'. This makes international society theory distinctive, for although it is clearly statist, its normative emphasis contrasts markedly with the starker version of realism. Neorealism, especially, has had difficulty in coming to grips with the idea of a system constituting a social entity with distinct normative elements. However, international society theory does not depart significantly from the realist emphasis on the state as the relevant unit or actor in the international sphere, and for this reason has often been placed within the realist camp. The emphasis on the state is reflected in the most widely cited definition of the international society idea put forward by Hedley Bull, but it also shows clear liberal elements through an equally important emphasis on institutions:

> [A] society of states (or international society) exists when a group of states, conscious of certain common interests and common values, form a society in the sense that they conceive themselves to be bound by a common set of rules in their relations with one another and share in the working of common institutions. (Bull, 1977, p. 13)

The English School conception of international society contrasts with the earlier articulation of the idea by Hugo Grotius. His more expansive notion of a 'great society of states', informed by a commitment to natural law principles as well as to positive law, explicitly included individuals and non-state groups. Moreover, in accordance with a genuine universal approach (in which the universe was not limited to Europe and Europeans), Grotius included non-Europeans within the scope of his international society (Keal, 2000, p. 67). By the time of the emergence of the English School, decolonization had ensured that non-Europeans were indeed included in the international society concept. Even so, the whole notion of international society and the legal, institutional and regulative basis envisaged for it, were undeniably European (or Western) in conception and therefore inevitably ethnocentric.

This general problem was recognized by English School theorists, leading some to adopt a 'pluralist' approach to the idea of international society as opposed to the 'solidarist' approach favoured by others. In this context, pluralism recognizes the fact that people, represented for practical purposes by states, have different conceptions and standards of justice, and that there is no universal yardstick for measuring and evaluating these. Each state must therefore be regarded as the repository of the values by which people live their everyday lives. This notion of pluralism tends strongly towards a form of relativism. Solidarism, on the other hand, recognizes the fact of pluralism or diversity, but does not endorse a strong norm of non-intervention when serious human rights issues are at stake. Therefore while states are certainly recognized as the most important units in international society, which is after all a society *of* states, and are crucial to maintaining world order, they are not immune from scrutiny of their human rights practices – or malpractices. 'Solidarism' may therefore be taken to refer to a certain 'solidarity of humankind' as well as the notion that it is possible to achieve a certain solidarity among states over standards of justice and morality that are universally applicable even in a pluralistic world. This accords with a liberal approach to the normative aspects of world order. In effect, then, the division between pluralists and solidarists reflects a tendency to a relativist/universalist bifurcation which is also reflected in turn in the communitarian/cosmopolitan divide in contemporary normative theory.

The pluralist approach to which Bull subscribed, and which tends more towards relativism, is best understood as an orientation to world order which assumes that although states are certainly capable of forming a society, it is one in which only a minimum of agreement is attainable (or necessary). The most important agreement is 'reciprocal recognition of sovereignty and the norm of non-intervention' (Dunne, 1998, p. 100). This means that states need not share substantive goals or values with respect to social life within the domestic sphere, nor any common view as to what constitutes justice. They need only agree on the need for order which is secured by a morally and legally binding code of coexistence (ibid.). This approach is within the bounds of traditional realism, but with an explicit normative position, and that is that world order constitutes a moral value in itself, as well as being a precondition for justice. The contrast with solidarism lies in the explicit concern of the latter approach with what goes on within the boundaries of states. Dunne points out, for example, that if a state fails in its duty to provide security for its own citizens, then from a solidarist viewpoint the society of states as a whole would need to consider suspending the principle of non-intervention: 'In contrast to the pluralist emphasis upon the rights and duties of states, this deeper level of solidarism places the rights and duties of individuals at the centre of its ethical code' (ibid.).

Neoliberal institutionalism shares some common ground with the English School, especially to the extent that it focuses on the conditions in which states may further their shared interests through establishing stable sets of norms and institutions (Adler and Barnett, 1998, p. 13). It has also contributed to integration theory, especially with respect to the EU, and to the analysis of international regimes defined by Stephen D. Krasner (ed., 1983, p. 3) in terms of principles and norms which in turn support rules and procedures. Current liberal theories of international institutions, like the idea of international society, do not repudiate the basic premises of realism. While they do not treat states as unitary actors whose domestic concerns are largely irrelevant to international issues, and obviously place much more faith in the capacity of institutions to ameliorate the condition of anarchy and contribute to a stable world order, they remain highly state-centric (see Martin, 1999; Slaughter, 1997).

The tensions between pluralism and solidarism, relativism and universalism, communitarianism and cosmopolitanism is nowhere more evident than in the principles and practices of the UN, which has been the major formal organ of global governance and world order for over half a century. In the post-Cold-War period, especially, the UN has struggled to strike a balance between the norms of non-intervention on the one hand, and a universalist concern with humanitarianism on the other. In short, the fortunes and failings of the UN, which may be regarded in some ways as the formal embodiment of the society of states, illustrates very well the various tensions mentioned above and with which international society theorists have long been concerned.

Global governance and the United Nations

The UN was the successor to the League of Nations and was set up under similar circumstances and with much the same purpose in mind. Born out of the experience of large-scale warfare, it was designed to prevent any such recurrence. Joseph S. Nye suggests that if the League of Nations had been designed to prevent the war that preceded it, then much the same can be said of the UN (Nye, 3/2000, p. 160). From the start, however, the UN enjoyed broader support in terms of membership than its predecessor. Whereas the League suffered from a distinct lack of enthusiasm among the most important players, especially the US, the UN, as mentioned above, started with fifty-one signatories at the San Francisco conference of 1945. It is also important to note that it was not dominated numerically by European states – all but nine of the original members were from other parts of the world, thus making the UN more 'global' from the beginning. It has remained the premier club for states, and indeed membership of the UN is regarded as an emblem of statehood. As decolonization took place in the aftermath of the Second World War, most former colonies acquired statehood and UN membership almost simultaneously (although statehood is not dependent on UN membership). By 1989 membership had more than tripled to stand at 159. The end of the Cold War and the collapse of the Soviet Empire brought about a further proliferation of sovereign states and by the beginning of the twenty-first century, the number of seats occupied by states in the General Assembly stood at 189.

With the deficiencies of the League in mind, the UN's designers attempted to devise a stronger system of global governance with a greater capacity for collective security to overcome the limitations and deficiencies that had rendered its predecessor largely ineffectual in preventing major war. For this reason, the most important and powerful body within the UN's central system is the Security Council, consisting of five permanent members with veto power – the US, the UK, France, Russia and China – plus fifteen rotating non-permanent members. The veto power of the permanent membership is potentially a significant impediment to action (something that plagued decision-making in the League), but is modified to some extent by the option to abstain from a vote. The permanent membership, incidentally, clearly reflects the outcome of the Second World War and is regarded by reformists as quite anachronistic. It also reflects an assumption that unless the most powerful states are given greater authority and status in the Security Council, then they are unlikely to remain committed to the organization as a whole. However, lack of commitment has been a problem. For example, although the US has been a key player from the start, elements within the US Congress – as well as US society at large – have been hostile both to the UN system as a whole and to some of its programmes. This has been reflected in the fact that the US has frequently been delinquent in its payment of UN dues. At other times, however, UN support has been vital for legitimizing US actions, such as leadership of Operation Desert Storm in the Gulf in 1991 and of the coalition against terrorism in Afghanistan in 2001–2.

The primary concerns of the UN with maintaining international peace and security, and therefore order, were complemented from the start by other normative and practical concerns. This is reflected in the significant number of programmes, funds and agencies set up under UN auspices. Among the best known are the World Health Organization (WHO), the UN Educational, Scientific and Cultural Organization (UNESCO), the International Labour Organization (ILO, which is a survivor of the old League), the UN Children's Emergency Fund (UNICEF), the UN Conference on Trade and Development (UNCTAD), the UN Environment Programme (UNEP) and the UN Development Fund (UNDP). Moreover, in drawing up a Universal Declaration of Human Rights, which was adopted by the General Assembly in 1948, and the covenants that followed, the clear implication was that it was not just the integrity of sovereign states with which the UN was to be concerned, but their individual inhabitants as well. As mentioned above, this concern for human rights has seen the UN adopt a more 'flexible' approach to humanitarian intervention in the post-Cold-War period, which would ordinarily be interpreted as undermining the principle of state sovereignty. However, if one looks again at the normative dimensions of 'internal' sovereignty itself, one can cast the humanitarian impulse to intervention in a slightly different light as upholding the moral basis of sovereignty in another sense.

The theory of sovereignty as articulated by Hobbes gave the sovereign, or ruler, virtually absolute authority over all the inhabitants of the state (whether described as subjects or citizens). But Hobbes also argued that people retained a fundamental right to self-preservation, since it was for this purpose that they had submitted to the sovereign authority in the first place. If the rulers of states today claim a 'right' to exercise unfettered sovereignty over the people within their territory, they do so on the grounds that they are carrying out a duty of care, in terms of security and protection, owed to these people. As suggested in the earlier discussion on human security, if sovereignty imposes any moral duties on states, it is surely the security and well-being of their own people. There are of course other arguments such as an appeal to 'national security' or 'national interest' over and above the rights of individuals or minority interests – a species of argument that relies on a utilitarian calculation of the greatest good of the greatest number. But in the end, there is a clear moral dimension to sovereignty claims that is directed to the well-being of all the inhabitants of a state.

To delve further into what gives any ruler or government its authority is beyond the scope of this discussion. But with respect to the question of humanitarian intervention into the 'domestic' affairs of a sovereign state, and its endorsement by the UN, it may be argued that the purpose of the UN in endorsing such actions is not to undermine the state as such, but to make it a *better* state in terms of its moral responsibilities to its own people. More in tune with the traditional objectives of the UN, however, is the argument that effective intervention and rehabilitation would make that state a better member of international society. And in the long run, this would contribute to a better quality of world order. In practical terms, it is not difficult to demonstrate the extent to which a state (or rather government) that behaves badly towards its own people generates a great many problems for certain aspects of world order – namely 'international peace and security' – the creation of large numbers of refugees or asylum seekers being an obvious example in the present period. This draws attention to the relationship between domestic and international order that has been emphasized by the UN over the last decade or so and which has provided a normative basis for many of its activities, especially peace-keeping. Michael N. Barnett (1995, p. 46) points out that: 'If the prevailing belief was once that international order was premised on balancing power and discounting domestic politics, there is now an increased conviction that domestic politics matters.'

In general, the UN is based essentially on the sovereign state system and is dedicated to the preservation of that system as the primary basis of world order. The norm of non-intervention reflects a pluralist position similar to that endorsed by English School theorists – as well as by more conventional branches of realism. Moreover, given that non-intervention is *the* norm, then intervention must always be regarded as exceptional, and something that always has to be justified. But the UN has also been concerned, implicitly at least, to turn a mere system into something resembling more of a society of states with solidarist underpinnings. This is reflected in the huge range of agencies, programmes and so on mentioned above. It is also reflected in the expectations that many people have of the UN when a crisis, either natural or human-made, emerges. Given the scope provided in principle by the Universal Declaration of Human Rights and the subsequent covenants, as well as the very different conditions of the post-Cold-War world, liberals would argue that the UN has the capacity as well as the duty to move beyond a minimalist notion of order to embrace one that embodies a measure of justice as well. The liberal economic order to be discussed next provides one version of justice. But it is one that has been condemned loudly by other critical voices.

Global economic governance and the liberal order

Justice comes in many forms, and economic or distributive justice is now one of the world's most important issues. As the brief survey of UN activities presented above shows, the organization has a number of key agencies involved in this area. More generally, the state of the international economy is also a matter that absorbs a huge amount of attention. The fortunes of the Dow-Jones and various other financial indexes, the rise and fall of currency values, commodity prices, trade balances, capital movements, interest rates and corporate governance – all feature as daily items of vitally important news. What is now termed the 'global economy' is a creature that can scarcely be governed or regulated in any strict sense of the word, but there are nonetheless some powerful institutions of global economic governance that shape this economy in various ways. In the post-Cold-War period, with a neoliberal order in the ascendancy, these institutions and the principles that underscore them have gained in strength.

Of the several important institutions set up in the wake of the Second World War, largely under US sponsorship and initially as part of a plan to rebuild Europe's economy, two – the IMF (which is part of the UN system) and the World Bank – remain to this day. Although their fortunes have fluctuated over the last half century, these two institutions are now among the most powerful and influential in 'governing' key aspects of the global economy as well as in dictating how the formal aspects of national economies are to be run in order to conform to the current liberal orthodoxy. One critic notes that the IMF is the linchpin in the implementation of the vision:

> Going beyond its original mandate to provide short-term balance of payments support, [the IMF] has coordinated with the World Bank in the 1980s and 1990s to promote fundamental structural and institutional reforms of national economies worldwide to better reflect the dominant vision of market-led rather than state-led development. . . . Beginning with Latin America and Africa in the 1980s in the context of the debt crisis, the IMF and World Bank turned their attention to the economies in transition post-1989, and more recently to East Asia. . . . Key components of IMF and World Bank packages include privatization of public services and public assets, liberalization of trade, finance and production, deregulation of labour and environmental laws, and the destruction of state activism generally in the public realm. (Thomas, 2002, p. 73)

Another highly important institutionalized process established in the early post-war years was the General Agreement on Tariffs and Trade (the GATT) which convened various rounds of multilateral trade negotiations over a period of several decades until it was finally succeeded by a permanent body in the form of the World Trade Organization (WTO) on 1 January 1995. At its inception the WTO was lauded as ushering in a new era by providing a legal and institutional base for international trade, a reliable contractual framework within which governments could formulate domestic trade policy and a platform on which trading relations among countries could evolve (Wilkinson, 2000, p. 55). The main objective of both the GATT and the WTO has been to liberalize trade with the further aim of promoting economic growth. Criticisms of the trade regime are varied, but many coalesce around issues of justice. According to Rorden Wilkinson (ibid., p. 140) a common complaint is that the WTO's framework empowers business, especially multinational corporations, to operate in ways that are 'detrimental to unskilled and semi-skilled workers, the environment and developing states'.

As mentioned above, all these institutions reflect the ascendancy of a neoliberal economic order, the ideology of which rests on the assumption that increased economic activity brings all-round benefits, to rich and poor alike. Richard Falk describes the 'characteristic vectors of neo-liberalism' as involving 'liberalization, privatization, minimizing economic regulation, rolling back welfare, reducing expenditures on public goods, tightening fiscal discipline, favoring freer flows of capital, strict controls on organized labor, tax reduction, and unrestricted currency repatriation' (Falk, 1999, p. 2). These matters form part of the debate over globalization considered in the next chapter. For the moment, it is important to note that not everyone is convinced of the general benefits to be gained from the prevailing economic order. After all, while many may now accept that capitalism is good at generating wealth, it nonetheless has a poor record on distributing it equitably. This is especially evident in the gap between rich and poor countries – often characterized as the North/South divide. A recent report noted that the richest fifty million, mostly from Europe and North America, have the same income as 2.7 billion poor people (Elliott, 2002, p. 19). But there has also been an increasing gap between rich and poor *within* advanced industrialized (capitalist) countries (see Thomas, 2002). This indicates a clear-cut need for a normative programme for international political economy (IPE) as part of the more general framework for studying IR in the contemporary period. More specifically, it has been suggested that what is needed is a critical, policy-oriented IPE 'attuned to a strong normative agenda of "order"; not an order that is simply a euphemism for the absence of open conflict and the presence of control, but one underwritten by strong policy impetus towards issues of enhancing justice and fairness under conditions of globalization' (Higgott, 2002, p. 97).

The issue of distributive justice has been an important focus for normative theory, and once again many of the debates have revolved around the themes of cosmopolitanism and communitarianism. In rejecting the communitarian notion of the 'morality of states', which effectively restricts the scope of moral obligation to the state sphere, Charles Beitz (1979) argues for a form of international social justice based on a redistributive principle that transcends state borders. The cosmopolitan moral principles on which this kind of approach is based have been further elaborated in relation to the concept of the 'basic needs' of humans which provide the essential basis for a theory of universal human rights (Shue, 2/1996), while 'quality of life' considerations have informed more ambitious cosmopolitan projects (see Nussbaum and Sen, eds, 1993). As with other aspects of normative concerns in international politics, the central theoretical tensions in debates about distributive justice revolve around the struggle by cosmopolitans to establish a universal standard of justice against which critiques of actual practices can be judged on the one hand, and the communitarian claim that such standards can only ever be grounded in the actual practices of particular communities.

The arguments for a critical IPE are attuned to the concerns of Marxist scholars discussed in chapter 3, and these have informed the approaches taken by critical theorists in recent years, especially in terms of the application of Gramscian ideas concerning hegemony to the analysis of world order. The best-known scholar in this field, Robert Cox, approaches conventional theories of world order via a method that questions the extent to which such theories are constructed on the basis of vested interests. Those who benefit from a certain construction of world order, whether they are conscious of it or not, tend to theorize that order as one that is 'natural' and therefore virtually unchangeable. This is linked to Gramsci's conception of hegemony in the sense that a prevailing order, since it is widely accepted as reflecting the natural order of things, tends to go unchallenged even by those disadvantaged by it. Cox further emphasizes the fact that theorizing can never be value free but is intimately linked with one set of interests or another. In addition, he has argued for a distinction between 'problem-solving theory' and 'critical theory'. The former, although not to be entirely discounted, tends to take the world as it is and simply explores how it can be made to function better. Critical theory, on the other hand, questions the very assumptions on which world order is based in the first place and whose interests are served by its maintenance. Cox's general approach to the question of theory and knowledge is summed up in his well-known remark that: 'Theory is always *for* some one, and *for* some purpose' (Cox, 1981, p. 128).

Global civil society and social movements

The term 'civil society' has a long and complex history in political thought and although it has its modern origins in social contract theory – exemplified by Hobbes's political theory of the state – the basic understanding that predominates today is owing to Hegel (whose influence on Fukuyama is noted in chapter 4). In its 'domestic' application, civil society is a sphere that stands beyond the family on the one hand, but which is distinct from the formal institutions of the state on the other. Hegel's thought did not render this distinction a rigid one, since the state was understood to synthesize the various elements within the political community, but it is common in the contemporary period to oppose the notion of civil society to the state. Thus civil society is now generally understood to denote that sphere of human interaction or association which stands apart from the formal activities and structures of the state.

The idea of civil society was popularized in the 1980s in such places as Poland, where the Solidarity protest movement was regarded as a manifestation of an emerging civil society specifically opposed to the communist state and seeking a measure of autonomy from it. A narrower meaning has also been adopted, largely by the NGO community, to refer more precisely to itself. Similarly, the term *global* civil society is often taken to refer to the community of international NGOs (sometimes called INGOs), as distinct from states, or organizations that function as the agents of states, or bodies founded on the state system such as the UN. INGOs include organizations such as Greenpeace, Amnesty International, Oxfam, Médecins sans Frontières, the Red Cross and the Red Crescent, the Scouts and Guides, Rotary International, the International Political Science Association, the Catholic Church, the World Council of Churches and so on.

A broad understanding of civil society, however, whether state-based or globally attuned, can include virtually any private company or association, unregulated marketplaces (including 'black' markets), clubs and charities as well as anarchist groups and illicit or criminal organizations whose activities range from the trafficking of arms, drugs and people to terrorism. Therefore, whereas many (including the community of 'good' NGOs) might want to attach an entirely positive connotation to the term, a more realistic understanding must include all manner of non-state (and anti-state) groups. But there is a certain class of NGO to which the UN 'recognizes' and grants consultative status. According to the UN's criteria, such organizations must have a recognized and democratically accountable executive and headquarters, they cannot be profit-making, they cannot advocate violence, they cannot be established by intergovernmental agreement, and they must support the aims and principles of the UN, including the principle of non-intervention. Some advocate a stricter set of criteria that would see only 'progressive' organizations admitted to consultative status rather than leaving it open to those such as the National Rifle Association (NRA) (Willetts, 2/2001, pp. 371–2).

As noted above, various manifestations of civil society activity have been linked to the phenomenon known as 'social movements'. These have also been described as 'alternative movements', 'new protest movements', 'new politics', 'new populism', 'neo-romanticism', 'anti-politics', 'disorderly politics' or 'counter-institutions', names which indicate a rupture or discontinuity with traditional forms of politics (Offe, cited in Camilleri and Falk, 1992, p. 206). A list of general movements (as distinct from specific organizations) that have both local (or state) bases and global networks would include the environmental movement, the feminist movement, the peace movement, the gay rights movement, the animal rights movement, various movements supporting indigenous rights, democratization and/or human rights as well as religious movements involved in social or political causes. As Camilleri and Falk note, 'this multiplicity of movements represents an extraordinarily diverse range of values, actors, issues and conflicts' (ibid., p. 206). More generally, it has been argued that the new social movements and the way in which they have been theorized have helped to reconstitute understandings of both the 'global' and the 'political' (Falk, 1991, p. 125). Once again, although most of the movements just mentioned may be associated with 'progressive' causes, others do not necessarily belong in this category. Islamic fundamentalism, for example, may be regarded as a broad-based social movement within the Muslim world, but it is hardly 'progressive'.

It has been argued that the relationship of many social movements to civil society is not defined by the boundaries of the sovereign state or by state-sanctioned actions (Camilleri and Falk, 1992, p. 211). This is certainly true of quite a few movements. Nonetheless, many social movements are state-oriented. For example, the various oppositional groups that made up the social movement that eventually succeeded in bringing democracy to South Korea in the early 1990s, and similar groups that saw the overthrow of President Marcos's dictatorship in the Philippines earlier in 1986, were clearly very much oriented to the domestic sphere. There was also the (unsuccessful) Pro-Democracy Movement in China that was brought to a partial end in 1989 with the Tiananmen Square massacre. Each of these movements is clearly state-oriented, yet at the same time they can be said to be part of a broader democratization movement, supported by various civil society groups (as well as by democratic governments), which has had a global presence since well before the end of the Cold War. It can also be argued that the collapse of communism in Eastern Europe and the former Soviet Union represented the net effect of a broad social movement whose component parts were essentially state-based and state-oriented. This, of course, has something to do with the fact that democracy is a form of government and governments are creatures of the state.

One of the best-known movements to arise in recent times, however, is certainly focused on the global sphere, and that is the amorphous collection of groups which together constitute the 'anti-globalization movement'. In some ways, it can be characterized as a 'movement of movements': the diverse groups that gathered to protest against the WTO in Seattle in late 1999, the IMF in Prague in September 2000, the EU summit meeting in Gothenburg in June 2001 and the G8 summit meeting in Genoa the following month represented causes ranging from the environment to Third World debt relief, as do the gatherings in various places on May Day each year. The most visible of the groups have been the revolutionary anarchists who invariably use violence in drawing attention to themselves and their cause. The common target of all groups, in one way or another, is 'global capitalism' and the increasing, and unaccountable, power of multinational corporations in the current world order. Whether one supports the basic principles of the liberal economic order or not, there is little doubt that the gross inequality within and between countries breeds trouble and that conflict arising from the maldistribution of goods and resources is likely to have serious security implications for world order in the future.

Regionalization and world order

Many discussions of world order and global governance, especially with respect to the economic dimensions, have obviously revolved around the phenomenon of globalization. This is widely viewed as one of the most significant features of the post-Cold-War landscape, and I explore the phenomenon and its implications for the state and IR more fully in the next chapter. But in the present period, regionalization (or regionalism, or regional integration) seems set at least to match globalization as a primary feature of world order. Regionalization is usually understood as an integrative process occurring at a supranational level, but within a certain geographical area. It is characterized by significant co-ordinated economic interactions and/or security dimensions, with accompanying social consequences. More specifically, regional *economic* integration has been defined as 'the process of reducing the economic significance of national boundaries within a geographic area' (Anderson and Blackhurst, eds, 1993, p. 1). Regionalization, however, is also believed to have a significant security dimension in terms of producing greater stability in the relations between neighbouring states.

Although a 'coming age of regionalism' was heralded more than ten years ago as 'the metaphor for our time' (Rostow, quoted in Fry, 2000, p. 117), in most parts of the world regional integration is still very much in an early stage of the process. The EU obviously represents the most advanced experiment, and one that has been a long time in the making. Forty-five years passed between the formation of the European Movement in 1948 and the Maastricht Treaty of 1992, which brought the EU into formal existence. Given that the deepening and widening processes are ongoing, the final destination of the EU remains unknown. Even so, there is little doubt that it is the most successful exercise in regionalization to date and the role model for other projects around the world. In the Asia-Pacific region there is the long-established Association of South-East Asian Nations (ASEAN), which was joined in 1989 by the Asia-Pacific Economic Co-operation forum (APEC). There is also the South Asian Association for Regional Co-operation (SAARC). In the Americas, apart from APEC which stretches across the Pacific, there has been the Central American Common Market (CACM) and the Central American Integration System (CAIS), the Latin American Integration Association (LAIA) – itself an offshoot of the Latin American Free Trade Association (LAFTA), the Common Market of the Southern Cone (MERCOSUR), the Caribbean Common Market (CARICOM) and the North American Free Trade Agreement (NAFTA). On the African continent there is the African Economic Community (AEC) and many sub-regional African associations including (among others) the Economic Community of West African States (ECOWAS), the Southern Africa Development Community (SADC) and the Arab Maghreb Union (UMA). The existence of these and other regional groupings and organizations gives some substance to the notion that the world is indeed approaching an 'age of regions'.

Another important development is inter-regionalism – itself a phenomenon that reinforces regionalization. A notable example is the Asia Europe Meeting process (ASEM), established in the mid-1990s. It was formed primarily to enhance economic relations but the process has also revealed some important cultural/ideological elements at work, especially on the 'Asian' side. The Asian membership includes most of the ASEAN countries plus the East Asian states of China, Japan and South Korea. Australia and New Zealand, although deeply enmeshed in regional trade and geographically contiguous with the ASEAN area, are not regarded as 'Asian' in a cultural sense and have therefore been explicitly excluded from consideration as potential members. Indeed, Malaysian Prime Minister Mahathir has said that if Australia wanted membership, it would have to apply to join on the European side even though this makes nonsense of the geographical underpinnings of regionalization. It has also been suggested that regionalism can sometimes be viewed as 'an anti-hegemonic strategy to control great power and particularly American or Western dominance' (Fry, 2000, p. 130). This has also been exemplified clearly in the promotion of Asian values as discussed above.

In summary, although regional schemes have existed for decades, the post-Cold-War world has seen a much stronger pattern of regionalization emerging. Certainly, the process of the EU's deepening and widening has been given a significant boost by the collapse of the strategic and ideological structures that supported bipolarity as a prime element in the world order of the Cold War period, as have emergent projects elsewhere. But are developments in terms of both regionalization and globalization – which are complementary rather than opposing processes – undermining the sovereign state? I discuss this general issue in more detail in the next chapter in the context of the debates about globalization. With respect to regionalization, however, it has been argued that at least in the case of the EU, sovereignty is now clearly divided and that 'any conception that assumes it is an indivisible, illimitable, exclusive and perpetual form of public power – embodied within an individual state – is outmoded' (Held, McGrew, Goldblatt and Perraton, 1999, p. 74). However, the EU model of 'pooling sovereignty' finds little support outside Europe. In South-East Asia, for example, the notion of 'regional society' has been applied to ASEAN, but it has been formulated explicitly to support a notion of community based on an almost absolute principle of non-intervention in the sovereign affairs of the member states (Fry, 2000, p. 122). This, in some ways, is a reflection of the fact that sovereignty has been achieved in the only relatively recent past and will remain jealously guarded for some time to come.

A fragmenting world order?

In chapter 4, which looks briefly at ethnicity and the deadly politics of identity in the context of post-Cold-War developments, I noted that, rather than seeing a new world order emerging along liberal idealist principles, many saw the rise of quite brutal 'new world disorder' instead. In terms of security and insecurity, the high incidence of ethnic conflict seems to have made the present period less stable, and less conducive to the maintenance of a peaceful world order, than the Cold War period was. As a significant number of problems in the present period have been due to the reconfiguration of the former communist world, it could be argued that the ensuing conflict and instability that has plagued parts of the former communist world since the end of the Cold War is a temporary phenomenon. But just as some serious problems for security and order – like those posed by Serbia – seem to reach some kind of resolution, others very quickly crop up to take their place. It should also be noted that ethnic conflict and identity politics have not simply emerged as a new phenomenon in the conditions of the post-Cold-War world. Various studies have identified well over 200 politicized ethnic groups as active in the period 1945–89; although not all of these have engaged in violence as a means to an end, around one hundred cases of armed conflict cited in the late Cold War period were over issues of autonomy or secession (Lawson, 1996, pp. 153–4).

The aim of many of those engaged in conflict with an ethnic dimension is the creation of a new state. It is for this reason that these groups are often described as 'ethnonationalist' – a term that fuses politicized ethnic identification with a demand for nationhood as embodied in formal statehood. This usually means the division of an existing state into at least two parts in order to satisfy the demand for full autonomy. Thus ethnonationalists among the Basques seek to split from Spain, the Quebecois from Canada, the Tamils from Sri Lanka, the Bougainvilleans from Papua New Guinea, the West Papuans from Indonesia, the Chechens from the Russian Federation and so on. Some Kurds seek a state of their own, which could involve hiving off parts of several existing states (Turkey, Syria, Iran and Iraq) to create a new state.

These movements are seen as fragmenting the state system 'from below' and to this extent have been regarded as a threat to world order. Former Secretary-General of the UN, Boutros-Ghali, once argued that if every ethnic (or religious or linguistic) group claimed self-determination in the form of independent statehood, 'there would be no limit to fragmentation, and peace, security and economic well-being for all would become ever more difficult to achieve' (quoted in McCorquodale, 1996, p. 9). His solution was to foster a greater commitment to human rights within states so that pressures for separatism would abate. This means, among other things, that although self-determination can be understood as a human right, it is not an absolute right, being limited so as not to create a threat to international security and not to infringe the rights and interests of 'other members of the international community' (ibid.). Generally speaking, then, the UN has not favoured the breaking up of states, although its approach is sometimes inconsistent. As noted above, some parts of the former Yugoslavia gained international recognition quite easily (if not peacefully), but independence for Kosovo is not on the agenda, at least for the present.

The postcolonial order

Problems of ethnic conflict have also been much in evidence in the former colonial world. As already emphasized, the period of decolonization following the Second World War created new states on the basis of boundaries originally constructed by colonial powers. In turn, this exacerbated the potential for ethnic conflict as many of these states contained diverse ethnic groups. Moreover, some boundaries actually split ethnic groups between states. But despite the potential problems of multi-ethnic states, the partition of former colonial states into more ethnically cohesive entities was resisted, and often resisted most strongly by postcolonial elites themselves. Those who had led nationalist struggles in the name of all the people of the former colonial state, and who ended up in positions of control, did not favour breaking up their newly acquired spheres of authority. The colonial order may have passed, but the postcolonial order of sovereign statehood throughout Africa, Asia and the Pacific was raised on its foundations.

An exception to this general rule was the partition of the Indian subcontinent in 1947, when India was redefined within its present borders while East and West Pakistan were set up as a single sovereign entity and as a predominantly Muslim state. The consequences, however, were probably more ghastly in terms of cruelty and bloodshed than was the case with any other country's path to independence. Partition was immediately followed by large-scale migration between the two newly created entities. Indeed there was a forced transfer of between fourteen and eighteen million people between the two countries. This was an exercise in ethnic cleansing in which not only millions of people were turned into refugees, but in which some two million Hindus, Muslims and Sikhs lost their lives as vengeful elements among all groups turned to murder, rape and a host of other abuses. In 1971 East Pakistan broke away to become Bangladesh – a very rare case of successful secession in the Cold War period. But the dispute over Kashmir continues to this day and still claims hundreds of lives each year. It has also brought two nuclear powers to the brink of open warfare.

Because postcolonial states are based on what often seems to be arbitrary boundaries determined by colonial bureaucrats, such boundaries are often described as 'artificial', especially as they did not follow a logic dictated by ethnic factors. This viewpoint, however, is also open to criticism, as to call a certain class of boundary 'artificial' assumes that there are other kinds of boundary separating (or enclosing) people that are somehow 'natural'. There is of course the sense in which a river, a mountain range, an ocean or some other feature may be regarded as forming a natural boundary. But to apply the term 'natural' to divisions among people on the basis of race, ethnicity, culture, language or some other marker of difference is another matter. As suggested before, to assume that something is naturally occurring is to cast it as permanent and unchangeable. Far from being fixed in this way, ethnic identity is best understood as situational, shaped by particular contextual factors. Indeed, ethnic groups can come and go, or their members can discard an identity and adopt another. Nor is ethnic identity necessarily tied to a political project, let alone one that demands a state to accommodate it. In addition, some members of the putative ethnic group, sometimes even a majority, do not support the cause (or tactics) of separatist groups. Not all Basques want to split from Spain; not all Sri Lankan Tamils support the separatist Tamil Tigers, and fewer than 50 per cent of

Quebec's population demands an independent state. So while it is true that the identity of particular groups can endure over very long periods, they are nonetheless subject to change, decline, renewal, abandonment and transformation depending on the political, social and economic forces at work in different circumstances and different periods. All this accords with theories emphasizing the socially constructed character of any political arrangement including the present world order.

Another phenomenon that must be mentioned in relation to the post-colonial order concerns the phenomenon of failed or failing states. The notion of failure here ranges from a chronic inability to sustain a reasonably secure social, political and economic environment for the citizens of the state, to those rare cases of genuinely collapsed states where virtually no legitimate governmental authority can maintain effective control of the central apparatus of the state (Zartman, ed., 1995, p. 1). From an external outlook, a failed state has also been described as 'utterly incapable of sustaining itself as a member of the international community' (Helman and Ratner 1992–3, p. 3). Another analysis takes up the concept of a 'weak state'. This has little to do with weakness *vis-à-vis* other states but rather with the effects of contending claims to power within the state. A distinguishing feature of weak states is therefore a problem with domestically generated threats to the security of the government rather than the state *per se*. Barry Buzan (2/1991, p. 101) says that the fact that some of these entities exist as states at all owes more to the simple fact of recognition by other states than to anything else. A specific cluster of internal problems that characterize weak states, including 'civil strife, political corruption, economic collapse, societal degradation, domestic collapse, human rights abuse, crumbling state infrastructure, and governmental failure' has also been identified (Langford, 1999, p. 61). In contrast with such gloom and doom approaches, which see yet more trouble looming for the state system and world order as a result of the apparently increasing symptoms of break-down in weak states (see Kaplan, 1994), others regard the state as an entity with a remarkable capacity for survival (Migdal, 1998). As discussed in the next chapter, this latter view contrasts with yet another body of contemporary literature which has little to do with the causes and consequences of failed states, but which has predicted, sometimes in a rather celebratory fashion, the decline of the state under the relentless forces of globalization.

CONCLUSION

This discussion of world order and global governance covers a selection of themes and issues from the idea of international society to the role of United Nations, the concept of global civil society as well as the impact of regionalization in the contemporary period and ongoing problems with postcolonial order and the ubiquitous phenomenon of ethnic conflict. One rather obvious conclusion to be drawn, especially in relation to the latter issues, is that world order at the beginning of the twenty-first century is in a state of flux. While the Cold War period can be seen in some sense as characterized by the spread and consolidation of the sovereign state system, as well as by a fairly rigidly polarized but nonetheless stable world order, the post-Cold-War period seems quite different in a number of respects, and much more unpredictable.

From an optimistic point of view, the end of bipolarity created a more flexible world order in which the opportunities for effective and productive regimes of global governance had been greatly enhanced. Through the UN, its various agencies and other bodies with a positive contribution to make, the lot of humankind as a whole seemed set for substantial improvement. These sentiments were expressed in much of the rhetoric about the possibilities for a new world order. Developments since the end of the Cold War, however, especially in relation to ethnic and religious conflict, failing states and the increasing gap between rich and poor countries, as well as thriving regimes of arms transfers, people smuggling and other such activities, have done much to mute the initial enthusiasm. In addition, some see the breakdown of bipolarity as having resulted not in the creation of a more egalitarian multipolar world, but a decidedly lopsided unipolar world order, the primary feature of which is US hegemony.

7

Globalization and the State

The discipline of IR was founded on key assumptions about the centrality of the sovereign state system to the way in which world politics was organized and conducted. It is one thing, though, to describe the structure of world politics in the modern period as revolving around the state system. It is another altogether to say that this is the only way things can be. And it is another thing again to say it is how things *ought* to be in a normative sense. As already stated, the privileging of the sovereign state and the state system has been vigorously challenged by alternative approaches to IR in recent years. These challenges have embodied not only a critique of state-centrism at the descriptive level, but also at the normative level, questioning deeply held assumptions about the state as a political community and the arena within which the 'good life' can be realized. But has the discontent among IR scholars with the state-centrism of their discipline, and its implications for normative issues, been superseded to some extent by the phenomenon of globalization in the contemporary period? If one is to believe some of the prophets of globalization, the sovereign state, which has long occupied pride of place in traditional IR theory, is destined to wither away under the impact of forces in world politics quite beyond the control of individual states and capable of transcending the state system altogether. Some would say that this has already occurred. Another view is that the state as described in IR theory has never really existed at all. These are among the issues and questions explored in this penultimate chapter.

The concept of globalization

According to one source, the term 'globalization' first appeared in *Webster's Dictionary* in 1961, marking 'the beginnings of an explicit recognition in the contemporary period of the growing significance of the world-wide connectedness of social events and relationships' (Kilminster, 1997, p. 257). A concept that had been developing over many years was thereby formally named. Once in the lexicon, its application became commonplace and over the next few decades it was used increasingly in relation to a variety of social, political and economic developments concerning the spreading network of relations around the world. Given its rather promiscuous application, it has also been described as 'the cliché of our times: the big idea which encompasses everything from global financial markets to the Internet but which delivers little substantive insight into the contemporary human condition' (Held et al., 1999, p. 1). The same authors, however, go on to say that clichés nonetheless do tend to capture certain key elements of lived experiences, and that the concept of globalization reflects genuine perceptions about the nature of the contemporary world. The understanding of the world reflected in the idea of globalization is one that is

> rapidly being moulded into a shared social space by economic and technological forces and that developments in one region of the world can have profound consequences for the life chances of individuals and communities on the other side of the globe. For many, globalization is also associated with a sense of political fatalism and chronic insecurity in that the sheer scale of contemporary social and economic change appears to outstrip the capacity of national governments or citizens to control, contest or resist that change. (Held et al., 1999, p. 1)

Although it is somewhat artificial to place the components of globalization into separate categories, it is nonetheless convenient for some aspects of analysis. One can therefore speak about distinct social, political and economic dimensions of globalization while at the same time recognizing that they are all interrelated. In broad social terms, globalization has been conceptualized as a 'process whereby the population of the world is increasingly bonded into a single society' (Martin Albrow, quoted in Kilminster, 1997, p. 257), and this is similar to the notion of the 'shared social space' mentioned in the quotation above. Politically, it may be understood as referring not only to the increasing enmeshment of people within the networks of global governance but also to the spread of more widely shared political values around the world, as manifest in a general trend to democratization. Economically, globalization is often seen to be at its most dynamic, especially since the collapse of communism; the increasing bias towards privatization and deregulation everywhere have given freer reign to market forces. In this sense, globalization may be seen to represent the triumph of capitalism. Given that capitalism also embodies certain social and political values, this economic dimension is clearly inseparable from the other ones.

Globalization is also generally conceived of as an historical process in which state or national institutions, authorities, actors and so on are increasingly bypassed in the course of interactions around the world, especially in the economic sphere.

> It is widely asserted that we live in an era in which the greater part of social life is determined by global processes, in which national cultures, national economies and national borders are dissolving. Central to the perception is the notion of a rapid and recent process of economic globalization. A truly global economy is claimed to have emerged or to be in the process of emerging, in which distinct national economies and, therefore, domestic strategies of national economic management are increasingly irrelevant. The world economy has internationalized in its basic dynamics, it is dominated by uncontrollable market forces, and it has as its principal economic actors and major agents of change truly national transnational corporations that owe allegiance to no nation-state and locate wherever on the globe market advantage dictates. (Hirst and Thompson, 2/1999, p. 1)

Among the important early writers on political economy who, despite profound ideological differences, nonetheless shared a conviction that capitalism was global in character and resisted containment or regulation within national borders were Adam Smith and Karl Marx. For Smith, the 'invisible hand' of the market was irresistible. For Marx, the global spread of capitalism was to be understood as an historical necessity. Beyond this, Marx is credited with being among the first to attempt the development of social-scientific concepts to deal systematically with 'the social regularities and patterns set in train by the rapidly extending global trade networks of his time' (Kilminster, 1997, p. 265). As discussed above, the global economic aspects of his theory of capitalism and imperialism were built upon by later theorists, including Lenin, while Wallerstein's world-system theory is among the best known in the postwar period. But Marx was also very much concerned with the concept of 'humanity' and his globalist ideas can be seen to synthesize certain Enlightenment ideas about this concept with a theory of the emerging global market, culminating in a 'utopian projection of a world communist society' (ibid.).

Marx is also the theorist who made famous the phrase 'the withering away of the state'. This condition was to be realized with the defeat of capitalism and the triumph of communism as a total political, social and economic system under which the apparatus of the state would no longer be necessary. But in the contemporary period, it is the triumph of global capitalism that has seen the state variously described as irrelevant, redundant, obsolete, powerless, in retreat, in decline or on its deathbed. I return to some of the arguments that underpin these diagnoses and prognoses shortly.

A brief history of globalization

Philosophical ideas about global interconnectedness are centuries old, especially in theories embracing a universalist approach to humankind. The Stoic notion of *cosmopolis* and the fact that major traditions of religious thought such as Christianity and Islam also conceptualize a community of humankind were mentioned earlier. These may seem remote from present-day discussions of globalization, and were certainly unrelated to theorizing about institutions such as the *sovereign* state and their place in a global system. They nonetheless embodied the essential idea of transcending particular political communities.

In Europe, exploration and 'discovery' led to knowledge of the finite world and, despite some stiff resistance from ecclesiastical authorities, also to the realization that this world was in fact globe-like in shape, not flat. A major practical step in the acquisition of geographical knowledge was taken with the first circumnavigation of the globe in the early sixteenth century. But it was the idea of humanity and the oneness of the human species that became especially important in global thinking – although it was hardly the main source of inspiration for explorers, merchants and colonizing agents. Nonetheless, ideas about humanity were embraced by various philosophers of the Enlightenment period, albeit in different ways, and continued to find expression in the universalist ideologies of liberalism and socialism that developed in the wake of the French Revolution.

The origins of the global economy also date back many centuries. One source says that they may be traced back to the sixteenth century, when European imperial expansion began, and that globalization today is simply a more advanced stage of the same process (Robins, 1999, p. 344). Another source locates the beginnings of the globalization of economic activity in the European Middle Ages, when systematic cross-border trading operations of a private corporate nature were initiated (Hirst and Thompson, 2/1999, p. 19), while another points to the fact that the ancient Babylonian and Roman empires practised forms of long-distance lending and trade (Scholte, 2/2001, p. 520). Others see the real take-off of economic globalization as occurring in the modern period with the development of international organizations, conferences, agencies, trade regimes and so on. An interesting historical checklist of certain key developments in several phases dating from this later period, and based partly on an historical study by the sociologist, Roland Robertson, has been drawn up by Robert J. Holton (1998, pp. 45–8) and appears below in a modified form, supplemented by an equally useful list of key events in the history of globalization drawn up by Jan Aart Scholte (2/2001, p. 18). It is by no means definitive, but does provide a good overview. For the first period from around the mid-eighteenth century to the 1870s, described as a phase of 'incipient globalization', the list includes:

- The increasing formalization of international relations through the consolidation of sovereign states and a state system, primarily in Europe and North America, with relations between states being embodied more frequently in bilateral and multilateral agreements.
- Increasing legal conventions and agencies directly concerned with the regulation of international relations. These included conventions of the treatment of the sick and wounded in war and the 1868 St Petersburg Declaration on the prevention of the deployment of incendiary substances in war.
- The development of international humanitarian regimes such as the World Anti-Slavery Convention of 1840.
- The beginning of international exhibitions such as the first world's fair held in London in 1851.
- The establishment of the International Committee of the Red Cross in 1863, one of the first ever international NGOs.

The second phase, from the end of the 1870s through to the 1920s, includes:

- The establishment of world time when twenty-four nations met in 1884, established Greenwich mean time and divided the world into twenty-four one-hour time zones.
- A significant increase in the number and speed of global forms of communication including the telephone, the telegraph and radio as well as the invention of what was to become the foundation of global transport, the aeroplane. The first transborder phone call was made between London and Paris in 1891 and the first scheduled transborder airline service commenced in 1919.

- The development of international competitions such as the modern Olympic Games (the first of which were held in 1896) and the Nobel Prize (1901).
- The inclusion of several non-European societies, such as Japan, in 'international society'.
- The First 'World War'.
- The institutionalization of the Gold Standard for the purpose of international monetary exchange, the massive expansion of capital export from Western countries and the beginnings of multinational companies.

A third phase from the 1920s to the 1960s saw, among other things, the formal entanglement of virtually the entire non-Western world in the web of globalization. The list here includes:

- The establishment of the League of Nations, followed by the more inclusive United Nations and its many agencies after the Second World War.
- The relative decline of Britain and the rise of the US.
- The effective globalization of the Cold War and its conflict over conceptions of modernity and world order.
- Decolonization (which includes the effective globalization of the sovereign state system) and the rise of the Third World voice in international affairs.
- Increased attention to the notion of 'humanity' following the horrors of the Holocaust and Hiroshima, as manifest in the Universal Declaration of Human Rights.
- The beginnings of global icons such as the launch of the 'Marlboro cowboy' in 1954 and the opening of the first McDonald's restaurant in 1955.

The final phase runs from the 1960s to the present, and is obviously ongoing. It includes:

- A greatly accelerated expansion of global communications, especially via electronic technology which allows virtually instantaneous transfer of information from one side of the world to the other. The first communications satellite was launched in 1962 and direct dial international phone calls were introduced in 1963. The first direct broadcast satellite was launched in 1976.
- The growing global influence of financial institutions such as the World Bank and the IMF, especially in terms of promoting liberal, market-oriented economic principles.

- The rapid expansion of foreign direct investment from Western countries in North America, Europe and East Asia as well as the increasing consolidation of the power of multinational corporations and international strategic business alliances. Technological advances also saw the first wholly electronic stock exchange system (the NASDAQ), launched in 1971.
- The end of the Cold War, which has created a more fluid (as well as uncertain) global system.
- A significant increase in the number of global institutions, INGOs and social movements and the rise of a global civil society.
- The introduction of the World Wide Web in 1991.
- A notable growth in consciousness of the environment as a global issue, as symbolized by the Rio Earth Summit in 1992.
- Further significant increases in transcontinental migration, including migration from the Third World to the First, which has brought with it a heightened challenge to monocultural nation-states in the name of multiculturalism.
- The growing impact of Islam in world affairs, which may be interpreted as running counter to globalization trends or, alternatively, as a form of globalization in its own right – and one that is challenging the hegemony of the West in the process.
- The growth of the 'anti-globalization movement', which emerged in tangible form around 1999–2000 and which coalesces around various 'global' events such as summit meetings of the WTO, the EU or the IMF and the celebration of May Day and so on.

All these developments and events have brought us to the point where globalization is believed by many to be the defining feature of the times.

Globalization versus the state

One of the main areas in which states – or, more specifically, their national governments – have been seen to be losing control is over the economic domain. This has been celebrated most enthusiastically by supporters of the liberal idea that the 'market knows best' when it comes to economic issues, and should be allowed to follow its 'natural' path. One well-known globalist has this to say about the utility of the state, especially *vis-à-vis* that of the market:

> The Nation-State has become an unnatural, even dysfunctional unit for organizing human activity and managing economic endeavour in a borderless world. It represents no genuine, shared community of eco-

nomic interests; it defines no meaningful flows of economic activity. In fact, it overlooks the true linkages and synergies that exist among often disparate populations by combining important measures of human activity at the wrong level of analysis . . . On the global economic map the lines that now matter are those defining what may be called 'region states'. The boundaries . . . are drawn by the deft but invisible hand of the global market for goods and services. They follow, rather than precede, real flows of human activity (Ohmae, 1993, p. 78)

This kind of approach has been described as a form of 'anti-political liberalism', a version of neoliberalism which celebrates the liberation of the global economy from the fetters of the state *and* of politics. In this vision, the state of the future will have little else to do except aid in the protection of the market system by maintaining law and order and upholding the rights of private property (Hirst and Thompson, 2/1999, p. 262). Objections to this rather extreme form of liberalism have come from both the political right and left. One view from the conservative end of the spectrum, which is also consistent with left critiques, sees clear dangers in this liberal rhetoric of globalization in that 'it reduces the scope of democratic political life to marginal adjustments in the management of market institutions', and 'closes off the political process to questions about the contribution made by market institutions to the satisfaction of human needs' (John Gray, quoted in Scott, ed., 1997, p. 1). Politics therefore needs to be reinvigorated in order not only to question the consequences of globalization for society, but also to defend society, where necessary, against the negative impact of market forces. And for a democratic socialist, concerted redistributive efforts (by states) must be made if the gross inequities created by capitalism are to be addressed. The convergence of traditional conservative and social democratic ideas in opposition to the anti-politics of the neoliberal economic project may at first glance seem rather odd. But the common ground in this instance is to be found in a normative commitment to communitarianism (although this is usually expressed in very different ways), against a form of economic universalism which is perceived as being almost completely devoid of any normative elements.

The 'end of politics' idea implicit in much globalist rhetoric about the decline of the state has also been critically discussed more specifically in terms of IR. While recognizing that the contemporary period of world politics has seen very significant changes in the context in which state power is exercised, Chris Brown emphasizes not only that states remain key entities in the sphere of world politics, but that political power has scarcely been abolished, much less politics itself. For these reasons, it would be foolish to discount all elements of realist theory. He also says that it is highly implausible to suppose that any forces in world politics will operate without reference to political power, as the more naïve proponents of market economics seem to assume. Furthermore, the future trajectory of globalization will be a result of political practice rather than of cultural or economic theory with 'the contingencies of political power' almost certainly having the last word (Brown, 1999, p. 57).

Other critiques of certain globalist views raise the issue of just how much substance there is in the assertion that the state has suffered a significant reversal in its fortunes under the impact of globalization. Without denying that the historical developments as sketched above have in fact taken place, one scholar working from an international political economy angle has argued that some very questionable assumptions underlie the current 'myth of the powerless state'. For one thing, contemporary globalists have grossly exaggerated the extent to which states have in fact exercised 'real' power in the past over their national economies (and other aspects of political and social life). The contrast between powerful states in the past and weak ones in the present is therefore highly misleading. Another unsustainable assumption concerns a certain logic in global capitalism which has (allegedly) forced convergence of national fiscal models around a particular norm – which is not in fact the case. There has also been a tendency among some political leaders – especially around the English-speaking world – to play up an image of 'helplessness', which is related to the 'weak state' assumption. This enables governments conveniently to evade responsibility for adverse economic developments at a national level (Weiss, 1998, pp. 189–94).

Another approach to the question of how globalization has impacted on the state separates out the traditional theory of sovereignty from the role and function of the state in other respects. Thus it is argued that:

> largely owing to globalization, the Westphalian system is already past history. The state apparatus survives, and indeed is in some respects larger, stronger, and more intrusive in social life than ever before. However, the core Westphalian norm of sovereignty is no longer operative; nor can it be retrieved in the present globalizing world. The concept of sovereignty continues to be important in political rhetoric, especially for people who seek to slow and reverse reductions of national self-determination in the face of globalization. However, both juridically and practically, state regulatory capacities have ceased to meet the criteria of sovereignty as it was traditionally conceived. (Scholte, 2/2001, pp. 21–2).

It is stressed, however, that although globalization has brought an end to the theory of sovereignty as traditionally conceived, it has not augured the demise of the state. Except for a few cases of state implosion (as in Somalia, for example) the state is as robust as ever in many respects (ibid., p. 22).

Contrary to this line of argument, another writer argues that the practical exercise of sovereignty has never matched the theory in any case. Like the argument about the 'myth of the powerless state' noted above, it is suggested that the extent to which states in the past actually enjoyed full sovereign powers is implicitly exaggerated in the globalist rhetoric of the contemporary period:

> One of the major difficulties with the argument that national sovereignty is under attack from globalization is the presumption that there was once a golden age when states possessed some kind of absolute control over their territory and the movement of resources, people, and cultural influences across their borders. This presumption is, however, very much a myth. National sovereignty, as it has evolved over the past 300 years or so, has always been more conditional than the myth implies. This is partly because the sovereignty of any one nation has usually depended on recognition by other nations, and partly because states have never been able, even if they wanted to, to achieve absolute control of transnational movements of people and resources across borders. (Holton, 1998, pp. 83–4)

It is clear from the above extracts that there are very different views on how sovereignty and the state, separately and together, have been faring under the impact of globalization, especially – although not exclusively – in relation to economic matters. However, these issues do not exhaust the general subject of the impact of globalization in the contemporary period. Another aspect of the subject concerns the fate of local or national cultural practices under the conditions of globalization. This also raises issues to do with modernization, 'Westernization' and/or 'Americanization' as well.

Culture and globalization

Although many discussions of globalization tend to revolve around economic issues, an equally interesting and important debate has been focused on the idea of an emergent 'global culture'. As already mentioned, one cannot neatly separate the various dimensions of globalization; the economic, the political and the social clearly overlap – although the economic is often privileged. In any event, there are obviously connections between culture and economics, culture and politics, culture and science and so on, such that one could argue that 'culture' is the master concept to which all others should be subordinate. This suggests that an economic system, or a political system, is simply part of an overall cultural system. On the other hand, one could also argue that where certain economic ideas and institutions become especially powerful, and the merchants are in the ascendancy, then cultural forces generally become subject to their influence. This kind of idea is behind at least some assumptions about the relationship between neoliberal economic forces in the contemporary world on the one hand, and local or national cultural forms on the other.

Three distinct approaches to these questions have been identified by Robert J. Holton – each operating under a different assumption. First, there are those who assume that under the present conditions of globalization, the dominant economic paradigm of global capitalism creates a version of cultural globalization in its own image. A second approach rejects this, viewing the prevalence of nationalism and ethnic politics as evidence of *resistance* to globalizing forces – both economic and cultural (and one could probably add political as well). Third, there is an outlook that repudiates both of these, promoting instead an approach that sees transnational cultural forms emerging, but which are not dominated by the logic of global capitalism (Holton, 1998, p. 161). Is it possible to accept, without fear of contradiction, that all three approaches have something valid to say about the contemporary impact of globalization? There is insufficient space here to address this question in depth, so I consider just a few general points relating to the various approaches.

The first concerns the notion of 'global culture', an understanding of which requires that one thinks once again about this thing called 'culture'. As noted in chapter 4, the concept of 'culture' is often taken to denote that which marks particularity or difference between human communities. In other words, culture is frequently taken as the key factor that differentiates one community from another and this makes their members into particular kinds of people. More specific definitions of culture, or explanations of cultural difference, may highlight language, religion, food rituals, dance, art, systems of distribution and exchange (i.e. economic systems), structures of political power and so on as elements in a total cultural package that makes each human community unique. Definitions of this kind are commonly found in anthropological literature, although not all anthropologists would necessarily endorse them. Even so, the idea of 'a culture' as something that is possessed by 'a community', and which in fact defines that community, is common enough.

'Global culture' is also understood as part of a universalizing and homogenizing trend that is set to transcend, or perhaps obliterate, the diverse local practices that make up the cultural map of the human world. This is what is implied in the view that global capitalism creates a version of cultural globalization in its own image – as evidenced by the ubiquity of Coca-Cola, Levi's and McDonald's or industrial icons such as Shell and Unilever, as well as the use of English as the dominant language of global communication and the Christian calendar as the global standard for dating. According to this view, the dominant products, companies and modes of communication that constitute the principal components of global culture are not actually drawn from all parts of the globe. Most (although certainly not all) have a particular origin, and that point of origin is the entity commonly referred to as 'the West'. With respect to the adoption of the birth of Christ as the point of reference for the universal dating system, it doesn't take much insight to recognize that this event has no special cultural significance for most of the world's people. As Kwame Anthony Appiah and Henry Louis Gates point out, it is therefore all the more remarkable that the story of the birth of Christ defines the dating system that most cultures use.

> And the way it happened is part of the story of how the military, economic and cultural expansion of the cultures of Christian Europe over the last five hundred years or so has led us into the first period of a truly global human history. Whatever their intentions, Europeans and their descendants in North America, a civilization we now call 'the West', began a process that brought the human species into a single political, economic, and cultural system whose details are, of course, the work of people all around the globe. (Appiah and Gates, 1999, p. ix)

These commentators further state that the present period is characterized by the existence of a global system of culture in which people from all over the world now participate, even though they may do so from different cultural positions. That cultural system, moreover, is increasingly *less* dominated by the West, or less Eurocentric than in previous periods (ibid.). Not everyone would agree with this fairly benign view of global culture and the role of the West in its formation, development and perpetuation. An alternative view of global culture may associate it more specifically with a form of globalization that is primarily about the expansion of Western technology, institutions, practices and values that can only end in Western cultural hegemony thinly disguised by the superficial incorporation of local cultural practices.

Another point to note is that although 'Westernization' as a form of global cultural change is a common general theme, especially with respect to the idea of 'cultural imperialism', it is actually global culture in the form of 'Americanization' that underlies many contemporary perceptions and fears. Interestingly, one author says that concerns about the phenomenon of Americanization have come not just from the Third World, or non-Western areas of the globe. They have also come from countries in Western Europe where, as far back as the 1950s and 1960s, 'there was a genuine fear, at least among the cultural elites, of the . . . hegemony of Coca-Cola culture' (Friedman, 1994, pp. 195–6).

The relationship between Westernization and/or Americanization on the one hand and modernity on the other is another issue. Modernity is often assumed to entail Westernization in one way or another. Indeed, the latter is sometimes posited as a necessary condition for modernity. But is it? Much depends on how modernity is conceptualized. The discussion in chapter 1 links modernity quite explicitly with a complex of scientific, political and social developments in Europe and North America. Developments in science and technology brought about industrialization and expanded forms of urbanization which in turn impacted on existing communities and lifestyles. The rise of the sovereign state system was another significant development but, by itself, did not necessarily bring about 'modern' politics. This was effected more through the rise of emancipatory ideas that rejected many aspects of traditional or religious authority, embraced a democratic agenda of political reform in national politics and promoted universalist notions of humanity.

When describing 'Western modernity', it is usually taken to include this entire package. The question therefore arises as to whether it is possible to dispense with some elements. For example, is it possible to have modernity without a liberal political and social system? The government of Singapore, which rules over one of the most 'modern' places in Asia, has attempted to achieve just that. Germany and Japan before the Second World War were authoritarian but also modern in the sense that they had advanced industrialized economic bases. The French postmodern philosopher Michel Foucault (1926–84) is well known for (among many other things) his assertion that the Holocaust was a product of modernity. Today, there are elements in many countries outside the West that want modernity in the technical, scientific and industrial sense, but without any liberal social and political elements. And they certainly don't want to become replicas of the US. Thus the desire for modernization is often qualified by a rejection of certain political and social values perceived as undesirable, as exemplified by the 'Asian values' debate as well as by discourses emanating from many Muslim countries. However, it is not beyond the bounds of possibility for countries to embrace liberal political and social institutions, as well as industrialization, without becoming clones of the US, Britain or any other Western country. It then becomes possible to speak of different expressions of modernity that do not dissolve into one amorphous category of global culture. Even so the perception of, and resentment towards, Western (and/or American) dominance in global culture is another source of anti-Westernism that clearly has implications for IR in the contemporary period, and possibly well beyond it.

Globalization, the state and normative theory

Proponents of cosmopolitan approaches to normative IR theory might be expected to welcome certain aspects of globalization, especially to the extent that it is conceptualized in terms of bringing humanity closer together through dispensing with, or at least softening, certain artificial political boundaries that have proved their divisiveness in more ways than one. Cosmopolitans have been especially critical of the extent to which the doctrine of state sovereignty, with its emphasis on non-intervention in the internal affairs of states, has been used as a shield behind which some state elites have perpetrated gross human rights abuses. They have been critical too, of the notion that morality depends primarily on a viewpoint derived from something called 'culture' and is not amenable to universalist schemes for the promotion of human rights and other goods. This does not mean that cosmopolitans see no value in community and the sense of identity, belonging and security it can provide. But acknowledging this scarcely means that the sanctity of state sovereignty, especially when deployed in conjunction with a pernicious doctrine of cultural relativism, can be defended in the face of gross acts which, in the more severe cases such as genocide, are described as 'crimes against humanity'. The force of this latter term is, rather obviously, one that relies on a thoroughly cosmopolitan morality that transcends all boundaries in its focus on humanity.

Communitarians, on the other hand, are persuaded that boundaries are an essential aspect of human existence, especially boundaries that reflect cultural divisions and provide an essential framework for community living, identity and values. Communitarian morality is therefore very much context-bound, which of course flies in the face of cosmopolitan theory. Even so, communitarians are hardly likely to argue that the privileging of 'culture' or particular 'community standards' over and above the concept of humanity and universal ethics could really excuse such acts as genocide, human sacrifice, torture as an instrument of a legal system and so on. Nor are all communitarians agreed that the boundaries of sovereign states in the present state system actually enclose genuine cultural communities that share a coherent value system, nor that the state is simply the community writ large. Few would deny that most states in the contemporary world contain a variety of groups that may be differentiated in terms of culture, ethnicity, religion and so on, leaving the equation of state with culture or, in the more common formula, state with 'nation' much more the exception than the rule. Even so, state boundaries have come to be privileged to a certain extent in communitarian discourses, perhaps on the grounds that state boundaries are tangible in a legal-institutional sense and do perform the task of enclosing and separating political communities.

Some of the issues arising from the cosmopolitan/communitarian divide in normative IR theory have been discussed above. Here, in thinking about normative theory and the state in the context of globalization, some additional matters arise. These concern the notion of responsibility – who bears responsibility and for what, and how far responsibility extends and, indeed, to what extent both the global and the local, the universal and the particular, are interdependent. One of the major issues on which these notions converge is that of the environment. Another is the situation facing refugees fleeing from conflict or threatened by natural disasters or simply unable to eke out a living in their homelands that is sufficient to feed, clothe, house and educate their families. The question for normative IR theory is what kind of ethic is most appropriately applied to issues such as these? Is it one based on the traditional sovereign state model of international relations and an inward-looking communitarianism, or must this be abandoned in favour of a 'global ethic' in tune with a cosmopolitan approach? Or is there a middle way that synthesizes elements of both? These questions provide a framework for thinking about some of the important normative issues that arise in the context of discussion about globalization and the state.

With respect to the environment, it is now an accepted fact that there are serious problems with pollution, land management, the availability of water and other natural resources all around the world and that these are likely to become much worse in the future unless urgent action is taken. But by whom? Since many environmental problems spread well beyond the local and are truly global in nature – such as global warming and climate change – it is much more difficult to fix responsibility and devise workable, practical solutions to cope with these. So while it is obvious that states, and local communities within them, may take responsibility for certain particular problems and work to remedy them as best they can, it is now a commonplace assumption that global action is required. It is further assumed that the will to achieve this can only be mustered by fostering a global ethic of responsibility. As one leading environmental ethicist argues, if people's loyalties stay confined to the local level, they will remain 'ludicrously inappropriate' to the challenges of global environmental management (Attfield, 1999, p. 23).

The most threatening of contemporary environmental issues is probably global warming, climate change and the state of the atmosphere generally. Virtually everyone has a stake in the effective management of the problem. Significant progress was made in relation to ozone layer damage in the late 1980s with international agreements to phase out the use of chlorofluorocarbons (CFCs) in the manufacturing industry. This required making alternative technologies available, especially in poorer countries. In turn, this meant that richer countries had to accept a responsibility for technology transfer. When the UN convened the Earth Summit in Rio de Janeiro in 1992, evidence of a developing global ethic seemed to be growing, but state interests and sovereignty were still very much in evidence. For example, some developing countries argued that it was their sovereign right to carry out commercial logging operations in forests, especially given their need to catch up in the development stakes. On the other hand the US, arguably the most 'developed' country in the world and certainly the one that consumes the most energy and resources per head of population, repudiated the Kyoto Protocol (1997) on greenhouse gas emissions at least partly on the grounds that the American lifestyle simply isn't up for negotiation. This also amounts to a repudiation of a global environmental ethic of responsibility in favour of a narrower 'national interest'. On the other hand, it must also be said that the US does not reject all forms of global ethics, as is evident in the present moral stance against terrorism.

The issue of refugees and asylum seekers raises similar questions about responsibility and the appropriate ethical response. Another commentator on normative IR theory considers some of the issues in terms of the cosmopolitan/communitarian debate. Observing first that official (and therefore conservative) estimates in the mid- to late 1990s put the number of refugees in the world at over sixteen million, he goes on to point out that many countries, and especially the wealthier ones, impose strict and generally unhelpful procedures for admitting political refugees, and usually refuse to accept 'economic' refugees. From a normative perspective, he points out that:

> Many cosmopolitans would argue that the rights of individuals to escape persecution or extreme poverty should lead to a relaxation of the tight frontier controls which are maintained. To be sure, such relaxation will have effects on existing citizens, who may prefer not to undergo possible reduction in economic well-being or not to have others who are not part of their community entering the country, and these preferences may well be seen as democratic justifications for not doing so. But it is not clear why these considerations should take precedence over meeting the basic needs of others. In many ways our

attitude towards refugees is a litmus test of how far we accept a cosmopolitan way of thinking and how far we retain a traditional communitarian approach. (Dower, 1998, p. 109)

A further key normative issue arising from the issue of refugees in particular, and what rights these men, women and children have in an international system of sovereign states that implicitly privileges a communitarian viewpoint, concerns the status that is conferred on people as citizens of particular states.

Rethinking political community

Many of the issues and questions that have arisen in relation to globalization and the state, and the various normative approaches to them, have prompted some serious rethinking in recent years about the nature of political community. It has been emphasized from the beginning of this book that the modern, sovereign, 'nation'-state form of political community is only one among a number of available possibilities. The importance of rethinking the utility and relevance of this form of political community has been pressed from a number of viewpoints, both practical and moral, and has been noted in the earlier discussion in this chapter in particular. Here I consider several responses to the call to rethink political community in the present period.

One current approach has come from a group of authors promoting the concept of 'cosmopolitan democracy'. Placing their analysis and arguments squarely in the context of globalization, the end of the Cold War and the widespread endorsement of democratic principles of rule, these authors argue that the time is ripe for the extension of democratic rule from the national arena to the international. They believe that there are, in any case, growing constraints in this era of globalization on the capacity of the state to take decisions (democratic or otherwise) without reference to the broader world: 'It seems reasonable to predict that political communities in the next millennium will have to come to terms with the developing process of globalization.' Accordingly, they must strive to 'adapt and consolidate democracy as a system of power management and to develop stable peaceful relations' (Archibugi, Held and Kohler, eds, 1998, p. 2).

In contrast to those viewpoints endorsing a capitalist economic/ technocratic solution as an ideal form of global balance, with perhaps a cartel of transnational corporations largely controlling the political agenda, or those who can see only the impending clash of civilizations on the global political horizon that requires strengthening defensive walls, the proponents of cosmopolitan democracy believe that there is a 'widely growing aspiration towards the development of a world order founded on international legality, the self-government of peoples and respect for universal rights' (Archibugi, Held and Kohler, eds, 1998, p. 4). The project of cosmopolitan democracy therefore proposes to meet these aspirations by engendering greater public accountability in the major global processes and structures of the contemporary period. This project differs from other cosmopolitan schemes in the extent to which it places democracy at the centre of the analysis of states, interstate relations and global issues. It does not, however, envisage a form of world government with a single centre of authority and states would continue to constitute an important part of the system, although not in their traditional sovereign form. In summary, the world is seen as consisting of 'overlapping communities of fate' whose organization must go beyond the mere coexistence of states:

> The case for cosmopolitan democracy is the case for the creation of new political institutions which would co-exist with the system of states but which would override states in clearly defined spheres of activity where those activities have demonstrable transnational and international consequences, require regional or global initiatives in the interests of effectiveness and depend on such initiatives for democratic legitimacy. (Archibugi, Held and Kohler, 1998, eds, p. 24)

Another cosmopolitan approach to the future of political community, which arises from critical theory, emphasizes the fact that throughout history these communities have generally owed their survival to the fact that the social bond between citizens and the state has not extended to aliens. 'Political communities endure because they are exclusive, and most establish their peculiar identities by accentuating the differences between insiders and aliens' (Linklater, 1998, p. 1). Therefore political communities are, in effect, systems of inclusion and exclusion characterized by social mechanisms which unite and separate, associate and disassociate, human beings. The moral implications of this are manifold. Andrew Linklater speaks in terms of 'moral deficits' which arise in relation to outsiders if citizens attach greater moral significance than can be justified to differences between fellow-nationals and aliens say, for example, by denying the outsider any rights in war. A moral deficit may also be evident *within* societies where minorities are prevented from preserving their cultural differences, or where dominant groups appropriate an unfair share of resources and opportunities (Linklater, 1998, p. 3).

Balancing the rights of culturally defined groups to maintain their sense of identity and community on the one hand, and the broader moral category of humanity on the other, is the task that Linklater and other critical cosmopolitan theorists have generally set themselves. Linklater goes on to make a case for the transformation of political community which entails the abandonment of the traditional Westphalian state. In doing so, he draws on many historical sources in political philosophy, including the writings of Kant. But it is the reference to Rousseau that strikes the most resounding chord in the context of the present discussion. Linklater notes that Rousseau defined the problem of modern politics in terms of the task of creating a society in which citizens could be as free as they had been in the state of nature. A related problem was how to create a society in which the ties binding citizens together did not at the same time make them 'enemies of the human race'. This captures, in short, the central problem of political community, and that is how to create communities or societies which do not subject aliens or minority domestic groups to the tyranny of unjust exclusion. This requires, above all, the recognition of all insiders and outsiders as moral equals (Linklater, 1998, p. 219).

CONCLUSION

Whatever other disagreements scholars of IR may have, and whatever their theoretical approach, there can be little argument that the sovereign state system has been regarded as the defining feature of international order throughout the modern period. As it spread throughout the world it displaced, subsumed or destroyed other forms of political community. Today there is scarcely a square inch of the earth's solid surface that isn't part of, or under the control of, a sovereign state. Even substantial areas of the world's seas, oceans and airspace have been assigned as belonging to this or that state. And whether or not people are generally conscious of it, states have played a significant role in organizing their lives from beginning to end as well as defining their basic political identities in the world.

However, the rise of the concept of globalization on the tide of rapid technological change, together with the end of the Cold War and its breaking down of political, social and economic barriers, has ushered in a period of serious rethinking about traditional political structures in world politics. One of the major issues canvassed in this chapter concerns the impact of these developments on the traditional sovereign state and the state system to which it has given rise. Are the state and the state system as they are known really in decline under the current forces of globalization? Or is the state simply in transition and already engaged in a dynamic process of adaptation as it has been for centuries? And if so, what practical and moral consequences will follow from it? If one regards the sovereign state model as something of a myth anyway, these may not seem to be especially important or interesting questions. On the other hand, if sovereign states are indeed the principal building blocks of a stable world order, as a number of prominent IR theorists have argued, then the question is a much more serious one. Given that the discipline has been virtually founded on the modern state and system, it certainly raises some interesting questions about its future.

8

Conclusion: A Postinternational World?

As an introduction to the study of IR, this book covers a selection of important themes, together with explanations of various theoretical approaches. Both the themes and the theories are presented in such a way as to provide the reader with an historical and contextual understanding of the subject, from the development of states in history and theories of human nature to contemporary issues such as security, world order and the phenomenon of globalization. A key focus of the narrative is on the state as a form of political community and, in particular, the centrality of the modern state to traditional IR theorizing. But I have also emphasized that the modern state's long-standing occupation of centre stage, in both theory and practice, has come under strong challenge in recent years. There is now an increasing emphasis in contemporary IR on activities that are not centred on the state and in fact operate quite independently of it. Non-state organizations are thriving as international actors in their own right. There are literally thousands of them, from those involved in international environmental issues, human rights, religious activities, peace advocacy to innumerable corporations and financial institutions, not to mention those involved in global racketeering of one kind or another. The activities of all these groups have a profound impact on world politics.

Such developments, along with the general impact of globalizing forces, may well lead one to believe that the very idea of 'international relations' as such is obsolete and that a stage of 'postinternational politics' has been reached. This idea has been put forward by James Rosenau, who argues that 'postinternational' is not just a fashionable label that simply fits in with all the other 'posts' going around, but a term that is genuinely needed to denote 'the presence of new structures and processes while at the same time allowing for still further structural development'. He explains further:

> Postinternational politics is an appropriate designation because it clearly suggests the decline of long-standing patterns without at the same time indicating where the changes may be leading. It suggests flux and transition even as it implies the presence and functioning of stable structures. It allows for chaos even as it hints at coherence. It reminds us that 'international' matters may no longer be the dominant dimension of global life, or at least that other dimensions have emerged to challenge or offset the interactions of nation-states. And, not least, it permits us to avoid premature judgement as to whether present-day turbulence consists of enduring systematic arrangements or is merely a transitional condition. (Rosenau, 1990, p. 6)

The idea of postinternational politics prompts a further question, and that is whether not only the stage of postinternational politics, but 'Postinternational Relations' has been reached in terms of how the field of study is itself constructed. In an essay entitled 'From International Relations to World Politics', R. B. J. Walker (1995) invites the reader, from a broadly postmodern viewpoint, to consider alternative understandings that are not circumscribed by the bounded territorial spaces occupied by the modern state. A similar message has come from some of the alternative approaches to the study of IR discussed in this book, namely critical theory, most versions of feminism and some variants of constructivism. The message is important, whether or not one believes that the modern territorial state is on the way out or not. As emphasized throughout this book, its importance lies in the fact that it encourages one to take on board that even the most familiar and apparently enduring structures and processes of world politics change – sometimes slowly but at other times rapidly and unpredictably. And they can change for better or for worse – 'progress' is not inevitable.

Another theme reinforced by alternative approaches is that there is more than one way of seeing the world. Varying images of world politics are purveyed not only via different theoretical approaches and models, but also by policy-makers and political leaders who will inevitably see things from very different angles, and who will act accordingly. In turn, political actions and events are experienced in different ways by different people depending on where and how they are situated, thereby giving rise to different interpretations, assessments and responses. Relative viewpoints do not derive simply from the particular position occupied by the observer in time and space. They may also derive from one's social position, which is why issues of class, race, gender and age must also be considered. Feminist scholars have contributed much to the understanding of how power can actually shape outlooks, some more compelling than others. In other words, political power has great efficacy in shaping and enforcing certain 'realities' for those who are subject to that power. Once the student of IR becomes aware of the very many different ways there are of seeing and experiencing the world, as well as how power is implicated in this, the subject matter becomes at once more interesting as well as more challenging.

Acknowledging the relativity of viewpoints contradicts significant aspects of the univeralism implicit in traditional approaches to IR, and this has fostered much of the dynamism evident in IR debates in recent years. However, I have shown that relativism also has its problems, especially in the field of normative international theory. The tensions between universalism and relativism have been clearly reflected in the cosmopolitan/communitarian debate. Although scarcely new to the IR agenda, these themes have become far more prominent in the post-Cold-War period as normative theory generally has gained a higher profile. This is due, at least in part, to the fact that important practical problems, such as the environment, sanctions, humanitarian intervention, refugee and asylum issues, have required a rethinking of many taken-for-granted assumptions about the morality of the sovereign state, the authority of state actors within both the domestic and international spheres and the linkages between these spheres.

These issues also indicate a broadening of the subject matter of IR itself as a 'new agenda' emerged in place of the old Cold War framework. Not all would agree that the end of the Cold War provided a significant impetus for change in the discipline and what it studies. Some would argue that the basic changes now seen as characteristic of the discipline in the post-Cold-War world had already occurred by the time the Berlin Wall came down. However, although there was indeed much discussion about new directions and approaches well before the end of the Cold War, I have taken the view that the collapse of bipolarity and superpower rivalry provided an important stimulus to the broadening of debates about the nature of world politics, what can be included in the scope of the subject matter, and how it should be studied.

As mentioned above, IR scholars are not the only ones to have been concerned with recent issues and developments in world politics. They have also drawn in economists, cultural and social theorists, historians, philosophers, geographers, anthropologists, students of comparative religion and psychologists – in fact just about the whole range of social science and humanities disciplines. The 'war on terrorism', for example, is clearly a prime issue for students of IR – but it is no less so for others. Indeed, in producing a well-rounded analysis of such issues, the student of IR will inevitably draw on other disciplines – from the history of colonialism and neo-colonialism in the Middle East, to the sociology of religion, the philosophy of 'just war', the geography and political economy of resources (water and oil) and so on. This suggests that the effective study of many issues in the contemporary world can scarcely be restricted to a single discipline. So for the student of IR, although the focus will remain on the political, thereby retaining an identity that is distinct from the more diffusely interdisciplinary field of international studies, an appreciation of what other fields of study have to offer and an ability to incorporate their insights is essential.

The new agenda also raises – although obviously not for the first time – questions about how one approaches the subject matter of IR. As discussed, positivist methodologies have been subject to a great deal of critical scrutiny. On the other hand, a social science that does not pay due attention to 'the facts' is hardly likely to be taken seriously. Dispensing with facts, however, is not what non-positivist methodologies or epistemologies are really about. Rather, it is how facts about the world are established and what is done with them that is at issue.

Finally, it should be clear that, despite the dominance of realism over the last fifty years or so, as well as the positivist methodological concern to turn IR into a value-free scientific enterprise, moral concerns cannot be regarded as largely irrelevant to the sphere of power politics. The original concerns of the discipline of IR as it emerged in the first part of the twentieth century were with the causes of war and the conditions for peace. In this sense, IR started out as a profoundly normative enterprise. Given the state of the contemporary world, with warfare of various kinds still plaguing the planet, these original concerns are obviously as crucial now as they were then. To these concerns have now been added a significant range of other issues. Whatever methods, approaches and theories have been adopted in the years since IR was first established as a formal discipline, and whatever else has been added to IR's subject matter, a normative purpose remains at its heart.

References

Adler, Emanuel, and Michael Barnett (1998), 'Security Communities in Theoretical Perspective', in Emanuel Adler and Michael Barnett (eds), *Security Communities* (Cambridge: Cambridge University Press).

Allen, John L. (4/2000), *Student Atlas of World Politics* ([Guilford, Conn.]: Dushkin/McGraw-Hill).

Anderson, Kym, and Richard Blackhurst (1993), 'Introduction and Summary', in Kym Anderson and Richard Blackhurst (eds), *Regional Integration and the Global Trading System* (New York: Harvester Wheatsheaf).

Appiah, Kwame Anthony, and Henry Louis Gates, Jr. (1999), *The Dictionary of Global Culture* (London: Penguin).

Archibugi, Daniele, David Held, and Martin Kohler (eds) (1998), *Re-Imagining Political Community* (Cambridge: Polity).

Ashley, Richard K., and R.B.J. Walker (1990), 'Speaking the Language of Exile: Dissidence in International Studies', *International Studies Quarterly*, 34, 3: 259–417.

Attfield, Robin (1999), *The Ethics of the Global Environment* (Edinburgh: Edinburgh University Press).

Barker, Sir Ernest (1959), *The Political Thought of Plato and Aristotle* (New York: Dover).

Barnett, Michael N. (1995), 'The United Nations and Global Security: The Norm is Mightier than the Sword', *Ethics and International Affairs*, 9: 36–54.

Baylis, John, and Steve Smith (eds) (2/2001), *The Globalization of World Politics: An Introduction to International Relations* (Oxford: Oxford University Press).

Beitz, Charles (1979), *Political Theory and International Relations* (Princeton: Princeton University Press).

Booth, Ken (1991), 'Security and Emancipation', *Review of International Studies*, 17, 4: 313–26.

Bowker, Mike (1997), *Russian Foreign Policy and the End of the Cold War* (Aldershot: Dartmouth).

Brown, Chris (1997), *Understanding International Relations* (London: Macmillan).

Brown, Chris (1999), 'History Ends, Worlds Collide', *Review of International Studies*, 25, December: Special Issue.

Brown, Chris (2002), 'The Normative Framework of Post-Cold War International Relations', in Stephanie Lawson (ed.), *The New Agenda for International Relations: From Polarization to Globalization in World Politics?* (Cambridge: Polity).

Bull, Hedley (1977), *The Anarchical Society: A Study of Order in World Politics* (London: Macmillan).

Bull, Hedley, and Adam Watson (eds) (1984), *The Expansion of International Society* (Oxford: Clarendon Press).

Burchill, Scott, and Andrew Linklater with Richard Devetak, Matthew Paterson and Jacqui True (1996), *Theories of International Relations* (London: Macmillan).

Burchill, Scott, Richard Devetak, Andrew Linklater, Matthew Paterson, Christian Reus-Smit and Jacqui True (2/2001), *Theories of International Relations* (London: Palgrave).

Buzan, Barry (2/1991), *People, States and Fear* (London: Harvester Wheatsheaf).

Camilleri, Joseph A., and Jim Falk (1992), *The End of Sovereignty? The Politics of a Shrinking and Fragmenting World* (Aldershot: Edward Elgar).

Camilleri, Joseph A., Anthony P. Jarvis, and Albert J. Paolini (eds) (1995), *The State in Transition: Reimagining Political Space* (Boulder: Lynne Rienner).

Carr, Edward Hallett ([1939], 1948), *The Twenty Years' Crisis 1919–1939: An Introduction to the Study of International Relations* (London: Macmillan).

Carruthers, Susan L. (2/2001), 'International History 1900–1945', in John Baylis and Steve Smith (eds), *The Globalization of World Politics: An Introduction to International Relations* (Oxford: Oxford University Press).

Cassells, Alan (1996), *Ideology and International Relations in the Modern World* (London, Routledge).

Clausewitz, Carl von ([1832], 1968), *On War*, ed. Anatol Rappaport (Harmondsworth: Penguin).

Connell, R.W. (1995), *Masculinities* (Berkeley: University of California Press).

Cox, Robert (1981), 'Social Forces, States and World Orders: Beyond International Relations Theory', *Millennium Journal of International Studies*, 10, 2: 126–55.

Dauvergne, Peter (ed.) (1998), *Weak and Strong States in Asia-Pacific Societies* (St Leonards: Allen & Unwin).

Deutsch, Karl (1957), *Political Community and the North Atlantic Area* (Princeton, Princeton University Press).

Devetak, Richard (1996a), 'Critical Theory', in Burchill, Scott, and Andrew Linklater with Richard Devetak, Matthew Paterson and Jacqui True, *Theories of International Relations* (London: Macmillan).

Devetak, Richard (1996b), 'Postmodernism', in Burchill, Scott, and Andrew Linklater with Richard Devetak, Matthew Paterson and Jacqui True, *Theories of International Relations* (London: Macmillan).

Donnelly, Jack (2000), *Realism in International Relations* (Cambridge: Cambridge University Press).

Dower, Nigel (1998), *World Ethics: The New Agenda* (Edinburgh: Edinburgh University Press).

Dunne, Tim (1998), *Inventing International Society: A History of the English School* (London: Macmillan).

Elliott, Larry (2002), 'A Cure Worse than the Disease', *Guardian*, 21 January 2002.

Evans, Graham, and Jeffrey Newnham (1998), *The Penguin Dictionary of International Relations* (London: Penguin).

Falk, Richard (1991), *Explorations at the Edge of Time: Prospects for World Order* (Philadelphia: Temple University Press).

Falk, Richard (1999), *Predatory Globalization: A Critique* (Cambridge: Polity).

Farrell, Theo (2002), 'Constructivist Security Studies: Portrait of a Research Programme', *International Studies Review*, 4, 1: 49–72.

Ferguson, Yale, and Richard W. Mansbach (1996), 'Political Space and Westphalian States in a World of "Polities": Beyond Inside/Outside', *Global Governance*, 2, 2: 189–213.

Frankel, Benjamin (1996), 'Introduction', in Benjamin Frankel (ed.), *The Roots of Realism* (London: Frank Cass).

Friedman, Jonathan (1994), *Cultural Identity and Global Process* (London: Sage).

Fry, Greg (2000), 'A "Coming Age of Regionalism"', in Greg Fry and Jacinta O'Hagan (eds), *Contending Images of World Politics* (Houndmills: Macmillan).

Fukuyama, Francis (1989), 'The End of History?', *The National Interest*, 16: 3–18.

Gaddis, John Lewis (1992–3), 'International Relations Theory and the End of the Cold War', *International Security*, 17, 3: 5–58.

Gaddis, John Lewis (1996), 'History, Science and the Study of International Relations', in Ngaire Woods (ed.), *Explaining International Relations since 1945* (Oxford: Oxford University Press).

Gamble, Andrew, and Anthony Payne (eds) (1996), *Regionalism and World Order* (London: Macmillan).

Gellner, Ernest (1986), *Nations and Nationalism* (Oxford: Blackwell).

George, Jim (1994), *Discourses of Global Politics: A Critical (Re)Introduction to International Relations* (Boulder: Lynne Reinner).

Goldstein, Joshua S. (2001), *War and Gender* (Cambridge: Cambridge University Press).

Groom, A.J.R., and Dominic Powell (1994), 'From World Politics to Global Governance', in A.J.R. Groom and Margot Light (eds), *Contemporary International Relations Theory* (London: Pinter).

Grunebaum, Gustave E. von (1953), *Medieval Islam* (Chicago: University of Chicago Press).

Hall, John A. (ed.) (1986), *States in History* (Oxford: Basil Blackwell).

Halliday, Fred (2001), *The World at 2000: Perils and Promises* (Houndmills: Palgrave).

Held, David, Anthony McGrew, David Goldblatt and Jonathan Perraton (1999), *Global Transformations: Politics, Economics, Culture* (Cambridge: Polity).

Helman, Steven R., and Gerald B. Ratner (1992–3), 'Saving Failed States', *Foreign Policy*, 89, winter: 3–20.

Higgott, Richard (2002), 'Taming Economics, Emboldening International Relations: The Theory and Practice of International Political Economy in an Era of Globalization', in Stephanie Lawson (ed.), *The New Agenda for International Relations: From Polarization to Globalization in World Politics?* (Cambridge: Polity Press).

Hirst, Paul, and Grahame Thompson (2/1999), *Globalization in Question: The International Economy and the Possibilities of Governance* (Cambridge: Polity).

Hobden, Stephen, and Richard Wyn Jones (2/2001), 'Marxist Theories of International Relations', in John Baylis and Steve Smith (eds), *The Globalization of World Politics: An Introduction to International Relations* (Oxford: Oxford University Press).

Hobsbawm, Eric (1994), *Age of Extremes: The Short Twentieth Century 1914–1991* (London: Michael Joseph).

Holsti, K.J. (1987), *The Dividing Discipline: Hegemony and Diversity in International Theory* (Boston: Allen & Unwin).

Holton, Robert J. (1998), *Globalization and the Nation-State* (Houndmills: Macmillan).

Howard, Michael (1983), *Clausewitz* (Oxford: Oxford University Press).

Huntington, Samuel P. (1993), 'The Clash of Civilizations?', *Foreign Affairs*, 72, 3: 22–49.

Jackson, Robert, and Georg Sørensen (1999), *Introduction to International Relations* (Oxford: Oxford University Press).

Jencks, Charles (4/1996), *What is Postmodernism?* (London: Academy Editions).

Kaldor, Mary (1999), *New and Old Wars: Organized Violence in a Global Era* (Cambridge: Polity).

Kaplan, Robert D. (1994), 'The Coming Anarchy', *Atlantic Monthly*, 273, 2: 44–76.

Katzenstein, Peter (ed.) (1996), *The Culture of National Security: Norms and Identity in World Politics* (New York: Columbia University Press).

Keal, Paul (2000), 'An "International Society"', in Greg Fry and Jacinta O'Hagan (eds), *Contending Images of World Politics* (Houndmills: Macmillan).

Kennedy, Paul (1988), *The Rise and Fall of the Great Powers* (London: Fontana).

Kenny, Anthony (1985), *The Logic of Deterrence* (London: Firethorn Press).

Keohane, Robert O., and Joseph S. Nye (1977), *Power and Interdependence: World Politics in Transition* (Boston: Little, Brown & Co.).

Keylor, William R. (1996), *The Twentieth-Century World: An International History* (New York and Oxford: Oxford University Press).

Kilminster, Richard (1997), 'Globalization as an Emergent Concept', in Alan Scott (ed.), *The Limits of Globalization: Cases and Arguments* (London: Routledge).

Kim, Woosang, and In-Taek Hyun (2000), 'Towards a New Concept of Security: Human Security in World Politics', in William T. Tow, Ramesh Thakur and In-Taek Hyun (eds), *Asia's Emerging Regional Order: Reconciling Traditional and Human Security* (Tokyo: United Nations University Press).

King, Preston ([1974], 1999), *The Ideology of Order: A Comparative Analysis of Jean Bodin and Thomas Hobbes* (London: Frank Cass).

Krasner, Stephen D. (ed.) (1983), *International Regimes* (Ithaca: Cornell University Press).

Krippendorff, E. (1982), *International Relations as a Social Science* (Brighton: Harvester Press).

Kuper, Adam, and Jessica Kuper (eds), *The Social Science Encyclopaedia* (London: Routledge).

Langford, Tonya (1999), 'Things Fall Apart: State Failure and the Politics of Intervention', *International Studies Review*, 1, 1: 59–79.

Lapid, Yosef (1996), 'Culture's Ship: Returns and Departures in International Relations Theory', in Yosef Lapid and Friedrich Kratochwil (eds), *The Return of Culture and Identity in IR Theory* (Boulder: Lynne Rienner).

Lau, D.C. (transl. and intro.) (1970), *Mencius* (Harmondsworth: Penguin).

Lau, D.C. (transl. and intro.) (1979), *Confucius: The Analects* (Harmondsworth: Penguin).

Lawson, Stephanie (1995), 'Introduction: Activating the Agenda', in Stephanie Lawson (ed.), *The New Agenda for Global Security:* Cooperating for Peace *and Beyond* (St Leonard's: Allen & Unwin).

Lawson, Stephanie (1996), 'Self-Determination as Ethnocracy: Perspectives from the South Pacific', in Mortimer Sellers (ed.), *The New World Order: Sovereignty, Human Rights and the Self-Determination of Peoples* (Oxford: Berg).

Lawson, Stephanie (1998a), 'The Culture of Politics', in Richard Maidment and Colin Mackerras (eds), *Culture and Society in the Asia-Pacific* (London: Routledge).

Lawson, Stephanie (1998b), 'Dogmas of Difference: Culture and Nationalism in Theories of International Politics', *Critical Review of International Social and Political Philosophy*, 1, 4: 62–92.

Lawson, Stephanie (ed.) (2002), *The New Agenda for International Relations: From Polarization to Globalization in World Politics?* (Cambridge: Polity).

Lenin, V.I. ([1917], 1996), *Imperialism: The Highest Stage of Capitalism: A Popular Outline*, introduction by Norman Lewis and James Malone (London: Junius: Pluto Press).

Linklater, Andrew (1996), 'The Achievements of Critical Theory', in Steve Smith, Ken Booth and Marysia Zalewski (eds), *International Theory: Positivism and Beyond* (Cambridge: Cambridge University Press).

Linklater, Andrew (1998), *The Transformation of Political Community* (Cambridge: Polity).

Linklater, Andrew (2/2001), 'Marxism', in Scott Burchill, Richard Devetak, Andrew Linklater, Matthew Paterson, Christian Reus-Smit and Jacqui True, *Theories of International Relations* (London: Palgrave).

Little, Richard (1995), 'International Relations and the Triumph of Capitalism', in Ken Booth and Steve Smith (eds), *International Theory Today* (Cambridge: Polity).

McCorquodale, Robert (1996), 'Human Rights and Self-Determination', in Mortimer Sellers (ed.), *The New World Order: Sovereignty, Human Rights and the Self-Determination of Peoples* (Oxford: Berg).

Maidment, Richard, and Colin Mackerras (eds) (1998), *Culture and Society in the Asia-Pacific* (London: Routledge).

Mann, Michael (1986), *The Sources of Social Power*, vol. 1: *A History of Power from the Beginning to A.D. 1760* (Cambridge: Cambridge University Press).

Mansbach, Richard W. (1997), *The Global Puzzle: Issues and Actors in World Politics* (Boston: Houghton Mifflin Co.).

Mapel, David R., and Terry Nardin (1992), 'Convergence and Divergence in International Ethics', in Terry Nardin and David R. Mapel (eds), *Traditions of International Ethics* (Cambridge, Cambridge University Press).

Martin, Lisa L. (1999), 'An Institutionalist View: International Institutions and State Strategies', in T.V. Paul and John A. Hall (eds), *International Order and the Future of World Politics* (Cambridge: Cambridge University Press).

Migdal, Joel (1998), 'Why Do So Many States Stay Intact?', in Peter Dauvergne (ed.), *Weak and Strong States in Asia-Pacific Societies* (St Leonards: Allen & Unwin).

Miller, David (ed.) (1991), *The Blackwell Encyclopaedia of Political Thought* (Oxford: Basil Blackwell, 1991).

Morgenthau, Hans J. (1948), *Politics among Nations: The Struggle for Power and Peace* (New York: Alfred A. Knopf).

Morrall, John B. (2/1960), *Political Thought in Medieval Times* (London: Hutchinson).

Nardin, Terry, and David R. Mapel (eds) (1992), *Traditions of International Ethics* (Cambridge: Cambridge University Press).

Navari, Cornelia (ed.) (1991), *The Condition of States* (Milton Keynes: Open University Press).

Nicholson, Michael (1996), 'The Continued Significance of Positivism?', in Steve Smith, Ken Booth and Marysia Zalewski (eds), *International Theory: Positivism and Beyond* (Cambridge: Cambridge University Press).

Nussbaum, Martha C., and Amartya Sen (eds) (1993), *The Quality of Life* (Oxford: Clarendon Press).

Nye, Joseph S. (3/2000), *Understanding International Conflicts: An Introduction to Theory and History* (New York: Longman).

Ohmae, Kenichi (1993), 'The Rise of the Region State', *Foreign Affairs*, 72: 78–87.

Onuf, Nicholas Greenwood (1989), *World of Our Making: Rules and Rule in Social Theory and International Relations* (Columbia: University of South Carolina Press).

Paul, T.V., and John A. Hall (eds) (1999), *International Order and the Future of World Politics* (Cambridge: Cambridge University Press).

Peterson, V. Spike, and Anne Sisson Runyan (2/1999), *Global Gender Issues* (Boulder: Westview Press).

Pettman, Jan Jindy (2/2001), 'Gender Issues', in John Baylis and Steve Smith (eds), *The Globalization of World Politics: An Introduction to International Relations* (Oxford: Oxford University Press).

Reus-Smit, Christian (1999), *The Moral Purpose of the State: Culture, Social Identity, and Institutional Rationality in International Relations* (Princeton: Princeton University Press).

Richardson, James L. (2000), *Contending Liberalisms in World Politics* (Boulder: Lynne Rienner).

Roberts, Adam (1991), 'A New Age in International Relations?', *International Affairs*, 67, (3): 509–25.

Robins, Kevin (1999), 'Globalization', in Adam Kuper and Jessica Kuper (eds), *The Social Science Encyclopaedia* (London: Routledge).

Rosenau, James N. (1990), *Turbulence in World Politics: A Theory of Change and Continuity* (New York: Harvester Wheatsheaf).

Ruggie, John Gerard (1998), *Constructing the World Polity: Essays on International Institutionalization* (London: Routledge).

Rummel, R.J. (1997), *Death by Government* (New Brunswick, NJ: Transaction).

Russell, Bertrand ([1946], 1979), *History of Western Philosophy* (London: Unwin Paperbacks).

Russett, Bruce (1993), *Grasping the Democratic Peace: Principles for a Post-Cold War World* (Princeton: Princeton University Press).

Sabine, George H. (1948), *A History of Political Theory* (London: George G. Harrap & Co.).

Sargent, Lyman Tower (1999), *Contemporary Political Ideologies: A Comparative Analysis* (Fort Worth: Harcourt Brace).

Schmidt, Brian (1998), *The Political Discourse of Anarchy: A Disciplinary History of International Relations* (Albany: State University of New York Press).

Scholte, Jan Aart (2/2001), 'Global Trade and Finance', in John Baylis and Steve Smith (eds), *The Globalization of World Politics: An Introduction to International Relations* (Oxford: Oxford University Press).

Scott, Alan (1997), 'Introduction: Globalization: Social Process or Political Rhetoric?', in Alan Scott (ed.), *The Limits of Globalization: Cases and Arguments* (London: Routledge).

Seager, Joni (2/1997), *The State of Women in the World Atlas* (London: Penguin).

Sellers, Mortimer (ed.) (1996), *The New World Order: Sovereignty, Human Rights and the Self-Determination of Peoples* (Oxford: Berg).

Shue, Henry (2/1996), *Basic Rights: Subsistence, Affluence and United States Foreign Policy* (Princeton: Princeton University Press).

Slaughter, Anne-Marie (1997), 'The Real New World Order', *Foreign Affairs*, 76, 5: 183–197.

Smith, Anthony (2001), *Nationalism* (Cambridge: Polity).

Smith, Steve (1996), 'Positivism and Beyond', in Steve Smith, Ken Booth and Marysia Zalewski (eds), *International Theory: Positivism and Beyond* (Cambridge: Cambridge University Press).

Smith, Steve (2000), 'The Discipline of International Relations: Still an American Social Science?', *British Journal of Politics and International Relations*, 2, 3: 374–402.

Spellman, John W. (1964), *Political Theory of Ancient India* (Oxford: Clarendon Press).

Stern, Geoffrey (2000), *The Structure of International Society* (London: Pinter).

Stohl, Michael, and George Lopez (1998), 'Westphalia, the End of the Cold War and the New World Order: Old Roots to a "New" Problem', paper read to the conference *Failed States and International Security: Causes, Prospects and Consequences*, Purdue University, West Lafayette, 25–7 February. Located at: www.ippu.purdue.edu/info/gsp/FSIS_CONF/stohl_paper.html.

Street, John (1997), 'Across the Universe: The Limits of Global Popular Culture', in Alan Scott (ed.), *The Limits of Globalization: Cases and Arguments* (London: Routledge).

Thomas, Caroline (2002), 'Developing Inequality: A Global Fault Line', in Stephanie Lawson (ed.), *The New Agenda for International Relations: From Polarization to Globalization in World Politics?* (Cambridge: Polity).

Tickner, J. Ann (1992), *Gender in International Relations: Feminist Perspectives on Achieving Global Security* (New York: Columbia University Press).

Tilly, Charles (1990), *Coercion, Capital, and European States, AD 990–1990* (Oxford: Blackwell).

Tow, William T., and Russell Trood (2000), 'Linkages between Traditional Security and Human Security', in William T. Tow, Ramesh Thakur and In-Taek Hyun (eds), *Asia's Emerging Regional Order: Reconciling Traditional and Human Security* (Tokyo: United Nations University Press).

True, Jacquie (1996), 'Feminism', in Scott Burchill and Andrew Linklater with Richard Devetak, Matthew Paterson and Jacqui True, *Theories of International Relations* (London: Macmillan).

UNDP [United Nations Development Program] (1994), *Human Development Report 1994* (New York: Oxford University Press).

UNESCO (1998), *World Culture Report: Culture, Creativity and Markets* (Paris: UNESCO).

Walker, R.B.J. (1995), 'From International Relations to World Politics', in Joseph A. Camilleri, Anthony P. Jarvis and Albert J. Paolini (eds), *The State in Transition: Reimagining Political Space* (Boulder: Lynne Rienner).

Waltz, Kenneth N. ([1954], 1959), *Man, the State and War* (New York: Columbia University Press).

Waltz, Kenneth N. (1979), *Theory of International Politics* (Reading, Mass., and London: Addison-Wesley).

Weiss, Linda (1998), *The Myth of the Powerless State: Governing the Economy in a Global Era* (Cambridge: Polity).

Wendt, Alexander (1992), 'Anarchy is What States Make of It: The Social Construction of Power Politics', *International Organisation*, 46 (2): 391–425.

Wilkinson, Rorden (2000), *Multilateralism and the World Trade Organisation: The Architecture and Extension of International Trade Regulation* (London: Routledge).

Willetts, Peter (2/2001), 'Transnational Actors and International Organizations', in John Baylis and Steve Smith (eds), *The Globalization of World Politics: An Introduction to International Relations* (Oxford: Oxford University Press).

Woods, Ngaire (1996), 'The Uses of Theory in the Study of International Relations', in Ngaire Woods (ed.), *Explaining International Relations since 1945* (Oxford: Oxford University Press).

Zartman, I. William (1995), 'Introduction: Posing the Problem of State Collapse', in I. William Zartman (ed.), *Collapsed States: The Disintegration and Restoration of Legitimate Authority* (Boulder: Lynne Rienner).

Zolo, Danilo (1997), *Cosmopolis: Propects for World Government* (Cambridge: Polity).

Index